D1564456

Great **Architects**
Les Grands **Architectes**
Große **Architekten**

Coordination and texts · *Coordination et rédaction* · Koordination und redaktion
Patricia **Bueno**, Marta **Eiriz**, Martha **Torres**.

Editorial Director · *Directeur Éditorial* · Verlagdirektor
Nacho **Asensio**

Design and layout · *Conception et maquette* · Design und layout
Carlos **Gamboa Permanyer**

Translation · *Traduction* · Übersetzung
Mark **Parent** (English)
Virginie **Leblay** (Français)
Frank **Eggers** (Deutsch)

Production · *Production* · Produktion
Juanjo **Rodríguez Novel**

Great **Architects**

Les Grands **Architectes**

Große **Architekten**

Contents / Index / Ínhaltsverzeichnis

Intro**duction**

The changes of century have always been decisive moments in the historical development of humanity. In one way or another, in the last decade of each century many of the transformations that have been "brewing" throughout the century, are carried out. In fact, this fact can be identified, or by disciplines, or by great interventions that, furthermore, involve the joint work of diverse professionals.

Like in many specialties, in architecture, this situation is also reflected. In this way, we find that great architects take it upon themselves to "close" a period with emblematic projects that, not only identify their work, but rather, also the fact of closing a period. Thus, many of these proposals are backed up by large scale plans which are sponsored by the country itself. Under these conditions, an interaction between architecture and the development of the cities is established: on the one hand, countries back their projects by means of "personal author" architecture, and on the other hand, the architects have become more and more international all the time as they project representative works in distinct places of the world. With all of these implicit or explicit intentions, many of the most important projects in the world have

been built, backed up by great archi-tectural offices.

In this book a revision is proposed of the architecture of the last decade of the twentieth century, by means of the most well-known professionals and some of their emblematic works. Although in many cases the projects chosen are of a great scale, some of minor scale have been introduced due to the fact that they have be-come significant within the trajectory of a specific author. All of this allows us to offer a double reading of a theme: the first allows us to present the projects of the last decade in or-der to show the world architectural panorama, and the second, to present some of the most significant works of an architect so as to offer a first vision of his professional development. The book is organized alphabetically by authors, which permits an immediate vision of his works.

With this selection and by means of architects with projects throughout the world, −ranging from authors so different such as Tado Ando or Michael Graves, to such significant architects such as Norman Foster−, the attempt has been made to offer a global vision of the "constructed facts" in the last decade of the twen-tieth century.

Intro**duction**

Les changements de siècle ont toujours été des moments décisifs dans l'évolution historique de l'humanité. D'une façon ou d'une autre, la dernière décade de chaque siècle est souvent le théâtre de la concrétisation des transformations générées par celui-ci. Ce phénomène peut être traité par disciplines ou grandes interventions, résultats du travail conjoint d'un ensemble de professionnels.

Comme dans de nombreuses disciplines, ce constat se retrouve dans l'architecture. Certains architectes ont en effet pour mission de "clore" une époque par des projets emblé-matiques, qui non seulement incar-neront l'œuvre du maître, mais mar-queront la fin d'une ère. Ainsi, nomb-re de ces projets s'inscrit dans des planifications à grande échelle pro-mues par les pays eux-mêmes. Dans ces conditions, une interaction s'é-tablit entre l'architecture et l'évolu-tion des villes: d'un côté, les pays renforcent leurs projets par une ar-chitecture "d'auteur", et d'un autre, les architectes s'internationalisent peu à peu grâce à des œuvres em-blématiques implantées dans le monde entier. Toutes ces intentions implicites ou explicites ont mené à la construction de projets parmi les plus importants au niveau mondial,

en collaboration avec de grandes agences d'architectes.

Ce livre propose de passer en revue l'architecture de la dernière décennie du xxème siècle à travers les artistes les plus reconnus et certaines de leurs œuvres phares. Bien que la majorité des œuvres présentées soient des œuvres à grande échelle, certaines réalisations plus modestes ont été intégrées par la signification qu'elles avaient prise au sein de la trajectoire d'un auteur donné. Tout ceci nous permet d'offrir une double lecture du sujet: la première est une présentation des projets représentatifs du panorama architectonique mondial de ces dix dernières années; et la deuxième, une présentation de certaines des œuvres les plus significatives d'un architecte donné, et par conséquence de son évolution professionnelle. Les artistes sont classés par ordre alphabétique, ce qui permet d'accéder directement à leurs œuvres.

Allant d'auteurs aussi différents que Tadao Ando ou Michael Graves, en passant par des artistes aussi importants que Norman Foster, cette sélection d'architectes et de leurs œuvres internationales cherche à offrir une vue d'ensemble des "événements architecturaux" de la dernière décennie du xxème siècle.

Einleitung

ie Veränderungen im Laufe der Jahrhunderte waren schon immer entscheidende Momente in der historischen Entwicklung der Menscheit. Auf die eine oder anderere Art und Weise haben viele Veränderungen, die im Laufe eines Jahrhunderts enstanden sind, immer im letzten Jahrzehnt stattgefunden. Man kann das tatsächlich festestellen, sei es in den verschiedenen Fachrichtungen, oder durch große bedeutende Eingriffe, außerdem an der Zusammenarbeit diverser Fachleute.

Wie in vielen Fachgebieten, spiegelt sich diese Situation auch in der Architektur wieder. Deshalb kann man festellen, daß sich große Architekten damit beschäftigt haben, eine Epoche mit emblematischen Projekten "abzuschließen", die nicht nur ihr Werk, sondern gleichzeitig auch das Ende einer Periode kennzeichnen. So wurden viele dieser Vorschläge von großzügigen Planungen unterstützt, die von den eigenen Ländern gefördert wurden. Unter diesen Bedingungen hat sich eine Wechselwirkung zwischen Architektur und Stadtentwicklung entwickelt: Einerseits unterstüzen die Länder ihre Projekte über die Architektur "des Künstlers" und andererseits internationalisieren sich die Architekten jedes mal mehr, in dem sie repräsentative Werke an verschiedenen Orten der Welt entwerfen. Mit all diesen impliziten oder expliziten Absichten

wurden viele der wichtigisten inter-
nationalen Projekte gebaut, mit der
Unterstützung großer Architektur-
büros.

Dieses Buch blickt über die bekann-
testen Fachleute und einige emble-
matische Werke auf die Architektur
der letzten Dekade des 20. Jahrhunderts zurück. Auch wenn in vielen
Fällen die ausgewählten Projekte
von grossem Maßstab sind, werden
auch einige kleinere vorgestellt, die
innerhalb des Werdegangs eines be-
stimmten Architekten von Bedeutung sind. All das erlaubt uns, eine
doppelte Lektüre über das Thema
anzubieten: Die erste, die die Projekte der letzten Dekade präsentiert,
um das weltweite architektonische

Panorama zu zeigen, und die zweite,
die einige der bedeutensten Werke
einzelner Architekten präsentiert,
um einen ersten Eindruck ihrer beruflichen Entwicklung zu bekommen. Das Buch ist alphabetisch nach
den Namen der Architekten sortiert,
so daß man ihre Werke schnell finden kann.

Mit dieser Auswahl von Architekten
mit weltweiten Projekten - die von
so unterschiedlichen Künstlern wie
Tado Ando oder Michael Graves
über so bedeutende Architekten
wie Norman Foster geht - wird versucht, einen globalen Überblick
über die "gebauten Fakten" der letzten Dekade des 20. Jahrhunderts zu
geben.

Tadao **Ando**

Tadao is a self-taught architect who learned his profession by travelling around the world and studying the works of masters like Le Corbusier. His minimalist style integrates the Japanese cultural tradition into contemporary architecture and explores the relationship between structure and landscape. The works of Ando give much importance to the spatial volume that forms create and they are guided by a true sense of order that inspires peace and spirituality.

Tadao Ando est un architecte auto-didacte qui apprit son métier au fil de ses voyages autour du monde et en étudiant les œuvres de grands maîtres tels que Le Corbusier. Son style minimaliste intègre la tradition culturelle japonaise à l'architecture contemporaine, et explore la relation entre structure et paysage. Les œuvres d'Ando privilégient les volumes des formes, régies par un véritable sens de l'ordre inspirant paix et spiritualité.

Tadao Ando ist ein autodidaktischer Architekt, der sein Handwerk im Laufe seiner Weltreisen und durch das Studium der Werke von Meistern wie Le Corbusier gelernt hat. Sein minimalistischer Stil integriert die kulturelle Tradition Japans in die zeitgenössische Architektur und erkundet die Beziehung zwischen Struktur und Landschaft. Andos Werke legen viel Wert auf die Außenansicht, die Formen schafft und von einem wirklichen Sinn für Ordnung bestimmt werden, die zu Frieden und Geistigkeit inspiriert.

1941	Born in Osaka, Japan.	*Naît à Osaka, Japon.*	Geboren in Osaka, Japan.
1962-69	Travels around the U.S.A., Europe and Africa. He studies architecture on his own.	*Voyage aux Etats-Unis, en Europe et en Afrique. Autodidacte en architecture.*	Bereist die USA, Europa und Afrika. Er ist ein Autodidakt in Architektur.
1969	Founds Tadao Ando Architect and Associates.	*Fonde* Tadao Ando Architect & Associates.	Gründet *Tadao Ando Architect & Associates*.
1991	Honorary Member of The American Institute of Architects.	*Membre honoraire de l'*American Institute of Architects.	Ehrenmitglied des *American Institute of Architects*.
1993	Honorary member of The Royal Institute of British Architects.	*Membre honoraire du* Royal Institute of British Architects.	Ehrenmitglied des *Royal Institute of British Architects*.
1995	Pritzker Prize of Architecture.	*Prix Pritzker d'Architecture.*	Pritzker-Preis für Architektur
1997	The Gold Medal from the Royal Institute of British Architects.	*Médaille d'Or du* Royal Institute of British Architects.	Goldmedallie des *Royal Institute of British Architects*.
1997	"Officier de L'Ordre des Arts et Des Lettres de Francia".	*Officier de l'Ordre des Arts et des Lettres, France.*	1997 *Officier de l'Ordre des Arts et des Lettres* in Frankreich.

Konferenzpavillon Vitra

1993. Weil am Rhein, Deutschland.

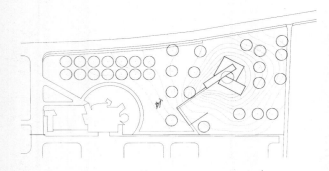

The principal theme of the project is the relationship of the building with the place and above all access to it. Tadao Ando decided to soften the impact of the building by not making it very tall so as not to break the tranquillity of the horizontal terrain. Part of its volume is underground and it is organized around a patio. This contraposition between solidness and emptiness enriches the interior space.

Le thème central du projet est la relation entre le bâtiment et le lieu, et surtout son accès. Tadao Ando a voulu adoucir l'impact du bâtiment; limiter sa hauteur pour ne pas agresser la tranquillité du terrain horizontal. Le volume est en partie sous-terre, et s'organise autour d'un patio. Ce contraste entre vide et solide enrichit l'espace intérieur.

Das zentrale Thema des Projektes ist die Beziehung zwischen Gebäude und Ort, und vor allem die Art des Zugangs. Tadao Ando hat sich entschieden, die Wirkung des Gebäudes zu besänftigen; ihm nicht zuviel Höhe zu geben, um die die Ruhe des horizontalen Geländes nicht zu stören. Ein Teil seines Raumes ist in der Erde vergraben und gruppiert sich um einen Innenhof. Diese gegensätzliche Position zwischen dem Soliden und der Leere bereichert den Innenraum.

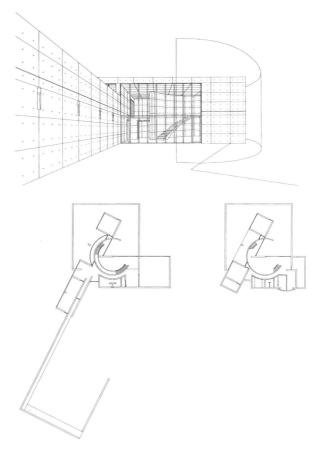

Three elements form the building: A rectangular volume parallel to the walls that delimit the lowered patio, another which penetrates the patio with an angle of 60 degrees, and a cylindrical volume which creates an emptiness and cuts the two rectilinear volumes.

Trois éléments composent le bâtiment: un volume rectangulaire parallèle aux murs qui délimitent la cour intérieure, un autre qui pénètre cette cour par un angle de 60 degrés, et un volume cylindrique qui crée un vide, et coupe les deux volumes rectilignes.

Drei Elemente bilden das Gebäude: Ein rechteckiger Raum parallel zu den Mauern die den versenkten Innenhof begrenzen, ein anderer, der in diesen Innenhof in einem Winkel von 60 Grad eindringt, und ein zylindrischer Raum der eine Lücke schafft und die zwei geradlinigen Räume kreuzt.

Chikatsu-Asuka Historical Museum

1994. Minami-Kawachi, Osaka, Japan.

"The purpose of the Chikatsu-Asuka Museum of History is to study and promote the Kofun culture. To integrate the museum with the tumulus, I conceived it as a staggered hill from which the visitor has a panoramic view of the necropolis. In the surroundings, plum trees, a lake and paths skirt the surrounding hills which integrates the museum into the landscape and facilitates the activities. The covered area, in fact, is a great staggered plaza which can be used for theatre productions, music festivals or performances. In the interior of the building, the exhibition areas are dark and the objects are exhibited just as they were found in the tombs. Visitors have the sensation of entering a tomb and immersing themselves in a past time". Tadao Ando.

"Le musée d'histoire Chikatsu-Asuka a pour but de diffuser et d'étudier la culture des kofun. Pour intégrer le musée aux tombeaux, je l'ai conçu comme une colline échelonnée, du haut de laquelle le visiteur a une vue panoramique de la nécropole. Des pruniers, un lac et des sentiers qui longent les collines environnantes intègrent le musée au paysage, et favorisent les activités. La toiture est une grande place échelonnée qui peut être utilisée pour des spectacles, représentations théâtrales, ou festivals de musique. A l'intérieur du bâtiment, les zones d'exposition sont peu éclairées, et les objets sont exposés tels qu'ils furent découverts dans les tombes. Les visiteurs ont l'impression de pénétrer dans un tombeau, et de plonger dans le passé". Tadao Ando.

"Das historische Museum von Chikatsu-Asuka widmet sich der Verbreitung und dem Studium der Kultur der Kofun. Um das Museum mit den Grabhügeln zu verbinden, habe ich es als einen abgestuften Hügel begriffen, von dem aus der Besucher einen Panoramablick auf die Nekropole hat. Im Umfeld Pflaumenbäume, ein See und Wege, die die umliegenden Hügel begrenzen. Sie integrieren das Museum in die Landschaft und begünstigen die Aktivitäten. Die Decke ist eigentlich ein großer abgestufter Platz, der für Theateraufführungen, Musikfestivale oder Performances genutzt werden kann. Die Ausstellungsflächen im Inneren des Gebäudes sind dunkel und die Objekte sind so ausgestellt, als wären sie in den Gräbern gefunden worden. Die Besucher betreten ein Grab und und tauchen ab in eine vergangene Zeit." Tadao Ando.

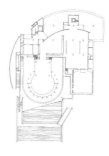

Artigues / **Sanabria**

CENTRO CULTURAL DE SANT CUGAT

The architecture of Artigues and Sanabria has been developed above all in the public sphere and it assumes civic obligations with the receivers of the projected works. Also they are assigned ordering functions and become models. In some of their works the architects have confronted sites with a very strong, heavy historical background and their intervention was limited by mediators. Nevertheless, they have also projected works which permitted a freer dialogue with the adjoining urban surrounding.

L'architecture d'Artigues et Sanabria s'est avant tout développée dans l'espace public. Elle représente un compromis civique avec les destinataires des projets, dont la fonction assignée se veut ordonnatrice et modèle. Pour certaines de leurs œuvres, les architectes se sont confrontés à des lieux profondément marqués par l'histoire, et une marge de manœuvre limitée par les alentours. Ils ont cependant également réalisé des ouvrages qui ont permis un dialogue plus libre avec l'espace urbain environnant.

Die Architektur von Artigues und Sanabria hat sich vor allem im öffentlichen Bereich entwickelt und übernimmt einen gesitteten Kompromiss mit den Empfängern der geplanten Werke, denen sie eine Ordungs- und Modellfunktion zukommen lassen. Bei einigen ihrer Arbeiten haben sich die Architekten Umgebungen gegenübergestellt, die sich durch eine starke historische Belastung und eine limitierte Nutzung der Grundstücksgrenzen auszeichnen, auch wenn sie Projekte entwickelt haben, die einen freieren Dialog mit der angrenzenden urbanen Umgebung erlauben.

	R. Artigues and R. Sanabria were born in Lleida, Spain.	Ramon Artigues et Ramon Sanabria sont nés à Lleida, Espagne.	R. Artigues und R. Sanabria sind in Lleida, Spanien, geboren.
	Degree in architecture from the *Escuela Superior de Arquitectura de Barcelona* in Barcelona in 1967 the former and in 1973 the latter.	*Diplôme d'architecte de l'Escuela Técnica Superior de Arquitectura de Barcelone respectivement en 1967 y 1973.*	1967 und 1973 Abschluss als Architekten an der *Escuela Técnica Superior de Arquitectura* in Barcelona, Spanien.
1980	They founded "Artigues and Sanabria", Architects	*Fondent Artigues & Sanabria, Arquitectos.*	Gründen Artigues & Sanabria, Architekten.
1991	Selected for the First Biennial of Spanish Architecture	*Sélection Ière Biennale d'Architecture espagnole.*	Erhalten eine Anerkennung auf der I. Biennale der spanischen Architektur
1995	Finalists for the Third Biennial of Spanish Architecture	*Finalistes IIIème Biennale d'Architecture espagnole.*	Finalisten der III. Biennale der spanischen Architektur
1995	FAD (Promotion of Decorative Arts) critics Prize	*Prix FAD (Fomento de las Artes Decorativas) de l'opinion.*	FAD-Preis (Förderung der dekorativen Künste)
1995	Finalists for the National Prize of Spanish Architecture	*Finalistes du Premio Nacional de Arquitectura de España.*	Finalisten des spanischen Nationalpreises für Architektur

Centro Cultural de Sant Cugat

1995. Sant Cugat del Vallés, Barcelona, España.

One of the biggest worries of the architects was to integrate the building into the city, in such a way that it afforded an urban landscape and consolidated itself as an important public place with the ability to structure a peripheral and dispersed area. The differences of height and size of the different spaces and halls enrich the volumetry of the building.

L'une des principales préoccupations des architectes était d'intégrer l'œuvre à la ville. L'ouvrage apaise le paysage urbain et s'impose comme un espace public majeur, capable de structurer une zone périphérique et désagrégée. Les différences de hauteur et de taille des divers espaces et salles enrichissent la volumétrie de l'édifice.

Eine der wichtigsten Aufgaben der Architekten war die Integration des Gebäudes in die Stadt, so daß es eine urbane Landschaft begünstig und sich als ein wichtiger öffentlicher Ort festigt, mit der Eignung zur Strukturierung einer zerstreuten Randzone. Die Unterschiede in Höhe und Größe der verschiedenen Räume und Säle bereichern die Volumetrie des Gebäudes.

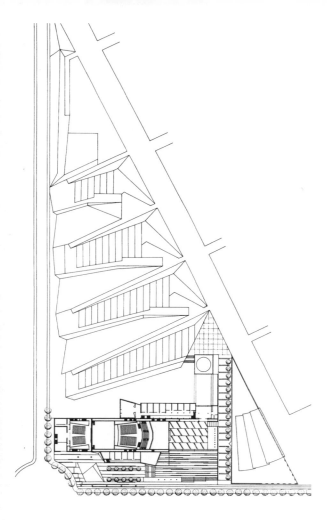

The profile of the building is constructed with curved lines and organic volumes which blend in with the shapes of the landscape.

Le profil du bâtiment est fait de lignes courbes et de volumes organiques qui se fondent aux formes du paysage.

Das Profil des Gebäudes ist mit kurvenartigen Linien und organischen Außenansichten gebaut, die sich mit den Formen der Landschaft mischen.

The plaza constructed in front of the building is an important part of the project as it gives it a detailed treatment which includes the broad stairs leading up from the street and the high lamp posts.

La place construite face au bâtiment, avec ses larges escaliers d'accès depuis la rue et ses hauts réverbères, joue un rôle prépondérant dans le projet, et lui offre un traitement détaillé.

Der Platz, der neben dem Gebäude gebaut wurde ist ein wichtiger Teil des Projektes, er gibt ihm eine Detailverarbeitung, inklusive weitläufiger Eingangstreppen von der Strasse aus und hohen Straßenlaternen.

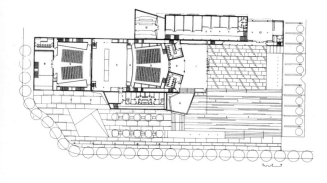

Baumschlager & **Eberle**

Karl Baumschlager and Dietmar Eberle are part of a generation of Austrian and Swiss architects whose architecture is characterized by an architecture which combines simple, unadorned, geometric shapes with a careful treatment of the skin of the building. Their works are treated like geometric compositions immersed in the landscape. It is difficult to distinguish between windows, balconies and marquees. All of these elements are interpreted from a rigorous geometry which dilutes them in the shape of the building.

Karl Baumschlager et Dietmar Eberle appartiennent à une génération d'architectes autrichiens et suisses caractérisés par une architecture qui combine des formes géométriques sobres et simples à un traitement soigneux de la couche des édifices. Leurs ouvrages sont traités comme des compositions géométriques fondues dans le paysage, de sorte qu'il est difficile de distinguer fenêtres, balcons ou marquises. Tous ces éléments sont interprétés à partir d'une géométrie rigoureuse qui les dilue dans la forme du bâtiment.

Karl Baumschlager und Dietmar Eberle sind Teil einer Generation von österreichischen und schweizer Architekten, die sich durch eine Architektur auszeichnet, die einfache und nüchterne geometrische Formen mit einer vorsichtigen Behandlung der Außenhaut der Gebäude kombiniert. Ihre Arbeiten werden als geometrische Kompositionen mitten in der Landschaft behandelt. Es ist schwierig, Fenster, Balkone oder Markisen zu unterscheiden. All diese Elemente werden von einer strengen Geometrie interpretiert, die sie in der Form des Gebäudes auflöst.

	Baumschlager was born in Bregenz, Austria, in 1956. Eberle was born in Hittisau, Austria, in 1952.	*Karl Baumschlager naît à Bregenz, Autriche, en 1956. Dietmar Eberle naît à Hittisau, Autriche, en 1952.*	Baumschlager ist 1956 in Bregenz, Österreich geboren. Eberle ist 1952 in Hittisau, Österreich, geboren.
	Baumschlager studied in the *Hochschule für angewandte Kunst Wien* (1975-1982) and industrial design with Hans Hollein (1975-78). Eberle studied in the *Technische Universität Wien* (1973-1978).	*Baumschlager étudie à la Hochschule für angewandte Kunst Wien (1975-1982) et le design industriel avec Hans Hollein (1975-78). Eberle étudie à la Technische Universität Wien (1973-1978).*	Baumschlager hat an der Hochschule für Angewandte Kunst in Wien (1975-1982) und Industriedesign mit Hans Hollein (1975-78) studiert. Eberle hat an der Technischen Universität Wien (1973-1978) studiert.
1982	They founded Baumschlager & Eberle & Egger studio.	*Fondent l'agence Baumschlager & Eberle & Egger.*	Gründen das Atelier Baumschlager & Eberle & Egger.
1984	They founded the Baumschlager & Eberle studio.	*Fondent l'agence Baumschlager & Eberle.*	Gründen das Atelier Baumschlager & Eberle.
1996	European Award for Industrial Architecture.	European Award for Industrial Architecture.	European Award for Industrial Architecture
2001	World Architecture Award from the World Architectural Magazine and the Royal Institute of British Architects.	*World Architecture Award de la revue World Architectural Magazine et du Royal Institute of British Architects.*	World Architecture Award der Zeitschrift *World Architectural Magazine* und des *Royal Institute of British Architects*

BETRIEBSGEBÄUDE HOLZ-ALTENRIED

1995. Hergatz, Deutschland.

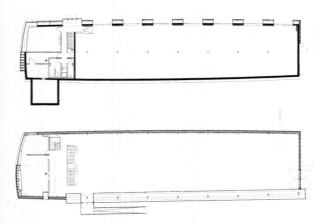

The structure of this building is like a box of curved walls made up of a series of plywood ribs. At the same time, it evokes the sensation of a boat beached in a post-industrial scene and the forms give you the feeling of poetic modernity, elegant and optimistic.

La structure de ce bâtiment est semblable à un volume de murs courbes formée par une succession de côtes collées en bois laminé, préfabriquées en bois d'épicéa. Cette réalisation évoque à la fois une nef primitive échouée dans un paysage post-industriel, et les formes d'une modernité poétique, élégante et optimiste.

Die Struktur dieses Gebäudes ist wie ein Kasten aus krummen Wänden, gebildet aus einer Folge von laminierten geleimten Holzrippen, hergestellt aus Rottannenholz. Das Gebäude erinnert gleichzeitig an ein primitives gestrandetes Schiff in einer postindustriellen Landschaft und an die Formen einer poetischen, eleganten und optimistischen Moderne.

Thanks to its geometry and its process of construction, the project suggests a handcraft, as if it were a handmade object.

Grâce à sa géométrie et à son processus de construction, cet ouvrage suggère le travail artisanal, s'assimilant à un objet fait à la main.

Über seine Geometrie und seinen Entstehungsprozess regt das Projekt eine kunsthandwerkliche Arbeit an, als wäre es ein manuell hergestelltes Objekt.

With this work, the architects pose questions regarding the present state of architecture. What we are dealing with, in reality, is an invitation to go into a poetic terrain by means of the compact and lyrical shape of the building.

Avec cette œuvre, les architectes s'interrogent sur l'état actuel de l'architecture. La forme compacte et lyrique du bâtiment est une invitation à s'engager sur un terrain poétique.

Mit dieser Arbeit haben die Architekten Fragen über den aktuellen Stand der Architektur in Betracht gezogen. In Wirklichkeit handelt es sich um eine Einladung, sich in ein poetisches Gelände über die kompakte Form und Lyrik des Gebäudes zu vertiefen.

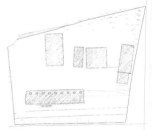

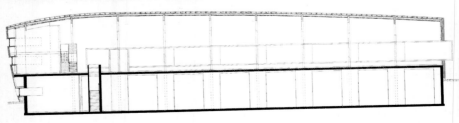

HAUS HÄUSLER

1995. Hard, Österreich.
Col: Rainer Huchler, Ernst Mader.

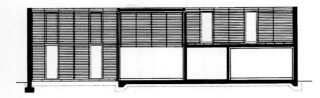

Häusler house has two skins: one of concrete and the other of wood. Between the two of them there are some open spaces that serve as interior patios. The house, designed by Bamschlager & Eberle, purposely differentiates itself from the buildings surrounding it. The majority of them are single-family dwellings, with double roofs, without any clear relationship among them nor with the landscape.

La maison Häusler a deux couches: une en béton et une en bois. Entre chaque couche s'ouvrent des espaces qui fonctionnent comme des cours intérieures. Cette maison conçue par Baumschlager & Eberle se démarque volontairement des bâtiments qui l'entourent, pour la majorité des maisons unifamiliales, d'architecture traditionnelle, aux toits à deux pentes, et sans lien clair ni entre elles, ni avec le paysage.

Das Häusler-Haus verfügt über zwei Außenseiten: Eine aus Beton und eine aus Holz. Zwischen den beiden öffnen sich einige Zwischenräume die auch als Innenhöfe dienen. Das Haus, das von Baumschlager und Eberle entworfen wurde, unterscheidet sich bewußt von den Häusern in seiner Umgebung; die meisten von ihnen sind Einfamilienhäuser in traditioneller Architektur, mit Spitzdächern, ohne eine klare Beziehung zwischen ihnen selbst oder der Landschaft.

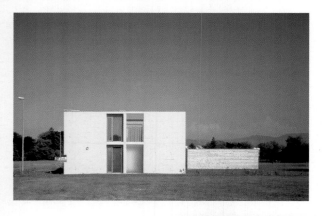

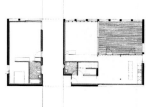

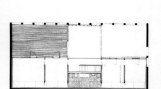

The architecture of this house springs from the relationship between the building and its surroundings, in spite of its apparent hermeticness and simplicity of construction.

L'architecture de cette maison naît de la relation entre l'œuvre et son environnement, en dépit de l'apparent hermétisme et simplicité de sa construction.

Die Architektur dieses Hauses ist aus der Beziehung des Gebäudes mit seiner Umgebung entstanden, trotz sichtbarer Verschlossenheit und Einfachheit in seiner Bauweise.

1994. Wolfurt, Österrreich.

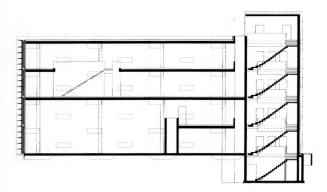

The place is defined by strong differentiating features which dictated the formal correspondence of the project. This means that each facade is in tune with its immediate surrounding. The compact character of the volume and the hanging facade system enable a very favorable basis in relation to the pre-established budget.

Le lieu se définit par des traits fortement différentiés qui ont exigé une parfaite adaptation du projet. Chaque façade fait écho à son environnement immédiat. L'aspect compact du volume, et le système de façade suspendue favorisent le respect du devis initial.

Der Ort entscheidet sich durch die sehr unterschiedlichen Züge die eine korrekte Übereinstimmung des Projektes nötig gemacht haben. Das bedeutet, daß jede Fassade sich in ihrer angrenzende Umgebung verbreitet. Der kompakte Charakter der Außenansicht und das hängende Fassadensystem erlauben von einer sehr vorteilhaften Basis in Verbindung mit dem vorher entwickelten Vorsschlag auszugehen.

The building basically consists of two rectangular spaces which show the texture of the materials like concrete, the blinds made of bare, unpainted wood, or the translucent glass.

Le bâtiment est essentiellement constitué de deux volumes rectangulaires, qui exposent les textures de matériaux tels que le béton, les stores à lamelles en bois brut ou le verre translucide.

Das Gebäude besteht im Wesentlichen aus zwei rechteckigen Außenansichten, die die Textur der Materialen, wie dem Beton, den Rolläden aus ungestrichenem Holz, oder lichtdurchlässigen Fenstern zeigen.

Günter **Behnisch**

Günter Behnisch's first projects explored the field of prefabrication in constructing schools. Starting from there and reaching world fame with the construction of the roof of the Olympic Stadium of Munich there was a long road in which the German architect searched for originality. He arrived to the conclusion that the latest building technology and modern materials afforded the necessary impulse to create innovative architectural options.

Les premiers projets de Günter Behnisch ont exploré l'utilisation de la préfabrication dans la construction d'écoles. Jusqu'à atteindre une renommée mondiale pour la construction du toit du Stade Olympique de Munich, il y a un long parcours pendant lequel cet architecte allemand a recherché l'originalité. Il est également parvenu à la conclusion que les dernières techniques de construction et les matériaux modernes apportent l'élan nécessaire à la création de possibilités architectoniques innovatrices.

Die ersten Projekte von Günther Behnisch erkunden Herstellung von Fertigteilen für den Bau von Schulen. Von dort bis zum Erreichen vom Weltruhm mit dem Bau des Daches des Münchener Olympiastadions ist ist es ein langer Weg auf dem der deutsche Architekt Orginalität gesucht hat und zu dem Schluß gekommen ist, daß die neuste Bautechnik und die modernen Materialien den nötigen Impuls zur Schaffung architektonischer innovativer Meinungen geben.

1922	He was born in Dresden, Germany.	Naît à Dresde, Allemagne.	geboren in Dresden, Deutschland.
1951	He completed his architecture studies in the *Technische Hochschule Stuttgart*.	Achève ses études d'architecture à la Technische Hochschule Stuttgart.	Beendet sein Architekturstudium an der Technischen Hochschule Stuttgart.
1952	He founded his own studio in Stuttgart.	Fonde son agence à Stuttgart.	Gründet sein eigenes Büro in Stuttgart.
1954	He founded *Behnisch & Partner*.	Fonde Behnisch & Partner.	Gründet Behnisch & Partner.
1982	Member of the *Akademie der Künste berlin*.	Membre de l'Akademie der Künste Berlin.	Mitglied der Akademie der Künste Berlin.
1989	He opens new office in Stuttgart, *Behnisch, Behnisch & Partner*.	Ouvre une agence à Stuttgart, Behnisch, Behnisch & Partner.	Eröffnet ein Büro in Stuttgart: Behnisch, Behnisch & Partner.
1995	Honorary member of the *Royal Institute of British Architects*.	Membre honoraire du Royal Institute of British Architects.	Ehrenmitglied des *Royal Institue of British Architects*.
1998	Fritz-Schumacher Prize from the *Alfred Toepfer Foundation*, Hamburg.	Prix Fritz-Schumacher de l'Alfred Toepfer Foundation, Hambourg.	Fritz-Schumacher-Preis der *Alfred Töpfer Stiftung*, Hamburg.

Deutscher Bundestag

1993. Bonn, Deutschland.

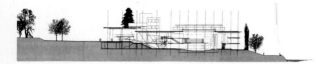

The Parlament occupies a privileged place: near the Rhine River and next to the banks of the river. Due to its considerable size, it was considered necessary to take special care so as not to distort the landscape.

The stairs of the building are similar to the elements of the landscape. Parallelly, Behnisch playfully connects the surrounding nature and the architecture: stairs which resemble a bird's nest, he establishes the continuity of an outdoor pathway with an interior way. The roof is practically transparent. Under a skylight, the hall is transformed into a small valley in the middle of a forest. Night and day, sunsets, the seasons, the winter snow, the lead gray of an autumn sky.... all of this comes into the building.

Le Parlement occupe un lieu privilégié: proche du Rhin et de sa longue promenade. Compte tenu de ses dimensions impressionnantes, il a fallu s'attacher tout particulièrement au respect du paysage. L'échelle du bâtiment reflète celle des éléments du paysage. Parallèlement, Behnisch établit des liens et des clins d'œil entre la nature et l'architecture: un escalier en forme de nid d'oiseau établit une continuité entre un sentier extérieur au bâtiment et un parcours intérieur. La toiture est quasi transparente, et sous la verrière, la salle se transforme en une petite vallée au milieu d'un bois. Le jour et la nuit, les couchers de soleil, les saisons, la neige en hiver, la couleur plombée du ciel en automne... envahissent tour à tour le bâtiment.

Das Parlament befindet sich an einem exklusiven Ort: direkt am Rhein und zusammen mit der langen Uferpromenade.Wenn man seine beachtliche Größe berücksichtigt, hält man es für notwendig eine besondere Aufmerksamkeit darauf zu legen, die Landschaft nicht zu verfälschen. Der Maßstab des Gebäudes ist dem der Landschaftselemente ähnlich. Parallel dazu entfaltet Behnisch Verbindungen und ein Zwinkern zwischen Natur und Architektur: Eine Treppe, die einem Vogelnest ähnelt, er führt eine Kontinuität zwischen einem existierenden Pfad außerhalb des Gebäudes und einem Gang im Inneren ein. Das Dach ist praktisch transparent. Unter der Dachluke verwandelt sich der Saal in ein kleines Tal mitten in einem Wald. Tag und Nacht, die Sonnenuntergänge, die Jahreszeiten, der Schnee im Winter, die bleierne Farbe des Himmels im Herbst... all das dringt in das Gebäude ein.

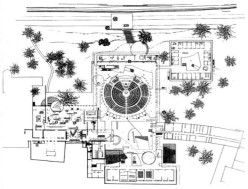

The building is not only transparent to the eyes, but also to movement. There is continuity, the space is flowing and open. This light aspect is due to, in part, its temporary character.

L'ouvrage n'est pas seulement transparent aux yeux, mais il laisse également transparaître le mouvement. Il y a une continuité, l'espace est fluide et ouvert. Cet aspect de légèreté est en parti dû à son caractère temporel.

Das Gebäude ist nicht nur für die Augen offen, sondern auch für Bewegung. Es hat Kontinuität, der Raum ist fliessend und offen. Dieser leichte Aspekt ensteht Zum Teil durch seinen temporären Charakter.

Ben **Van Berkel**

Many of his works are based on abstract concepts represented by diagrams that study the pressures that a project can be under: from the conditioning factors of the place all the way to technology. In effect, the reflection of this union of forces in movement is attempted whether it be by means of the lines of the facade or the formal image of the whole. He makes use of assymetries, the variety of materials or transparencies that allow the conceptual dynamic which originated them, to be perceived.

Bon nombre de ses œuvres reposent sur des concepts abstraits représentés sous forme de diagrammes qui étudient les pressions exercées sur un projet, des composantes du lieu à la technologie. En effet, il s'agit de refléter cette union des forces en mouvement, que ce soit dans les lignes de la façade ou dans l'image formelle de l'ensemble. C'est pourquoi il fait appel aux asymétries, à des matériaux divers ou à des transparences qui permettent de percevoir la dynamique conceptuelle qui en est à l'origine.

Viele seiner Arbeiten basieren auf abstrakten Konzepten, die in Diagrammen dargestellt sind, welche den Druck studieren, dem ein Projekt unterworfen sein kann: von den ortsbedingten Faktoren bis zur Technologie. Tatsächlich versucht er sich diese Verbindung von Bewegungskräften vorzustellen, sei es über die Linen der Fassade oder das formale Bild des Komplexes. Er wendet sich sich an die Asymetrie, an die Vielfalt der Materialien oder an die Transparenz, die es erlaubt, die begriffliche Dynamik wahrzunehmen, die sie hervorrufen.

1957	Born in Utrecht, The Netherlands.	*Naît à Utrecht, Pays-Bas.*	Geboren in Utrecht, Niederlande
1987	He completed his studies at the *Architectural Association School* in London.	*Achève ses études à l'Architectural Association School de Londres.*	Beenet sein Studium in der *Architectural Association School* in London
1988	He founded *Van Berkel & Bos Architectuurbureau* studio together with Caroline Bos.	*Fonde en collaboration avec Caroline Bos l'agence* Van Berkel & Bos Architectuur Bureau.	Gründet zusammen mit Caroline Bos das Büro *Van Berkel & Bos Architectuurbureau*
1991	Charlotte Köhler Prize.	*Prix Charlotte Köhler.*	Charlotte-Köhler-Preis
1996-99	He directs the Diploma Unit 4 of urban studies at the *Architectural Association School* in London.	*Dirige le Diplôme Unit 4 d'études urbaines de l'*Architectural Association School *de Londres.*	Leitet die *Diploma Unit 4* der urbanen Studien der *Architectural Association School* in London.
1997	Honorary member of the *Bund Deutscher Architekten.*	*Membre honoraire du* Bund Deutscher Architekten.	Ehrenmitglied des *Bundes Deutscher Architekten.*
1998	Together with Caroline Boss set up a second office, *Un Studio.*	*Fonde avec Caroline Bos une nouvelle filiale,* UN Studio.	Gründet zusammen mit Caroline Bos ein zweites Büro, *UN Studio.*

Vroom & Dreesman Shopping Center

1996. Emmen, The Netherlands.

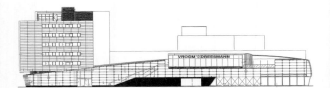

The building of the new warehouses of Vroom & Dreesmann is the result of a complete remodeling of an old renovation of the sixties. Van Berkel's project adds an apartment building, reorganizes the whole complex and completely changes the facade, by replacing it with an enveloping skin which becomes a key element which provides a new unity to the image of the building.

Le bâtiment des nouveaux magasins Vroom & Dreesmann est le résultat d'une redistribution globale de l'ancienne ordonnance des années soixante.
Le projet de Van Berkel ajoute un immeuble d'habitations, réorganise l'ensemble et modifie radicalement la façade. Elle est remplacée par une couche enveloppante, qui deviendra un élément clé apportant une nouvelle unité à l'image de l'édifice.

Das Gebäude des neuen Kaufhauses *Vroom & Dreesmann* ist das Ergebnis einer globalen Remodellierung einer alten Raumordnung aus den 60 er Jahren. Das Projekt von Van Berkel fügt ein Appartementhaus hinzu, reorganisiert den gesamten Komplex und verändert die komplette Fassade, ersetzt sie durch eine verhüllende Haut, die sich in das Schlüsselelement verwandelt, das eine neue Einheit an das Gesamtbild des Gebäudes anpasst.

The complex is characterized by an assembly of pieces: the floor moulding of the ground floor, in some cases open; the volume of the first floor, an enormous flattened piece of glass; a five-storey tower, a three-storey prismatic body and a few other bodies that protrude out over the glass piece.

L'œuvre se caractérise par un assemblage de pièces: le soubassement du rez-de-chaussée, parfois ouvert; le volume du premier étage, immense pièce vitrée; une tour de cinq étages, un corps prismatique de trois étages, et un autre corps qui surplombe la pièce vitrée.

Der Komplex zeichnet sich durch eine Verbindung von Teilen aus: der Sockel des Erdgeschosses, das in einigen Fällen offen ist; der Raum im ersten Stock ist flaches Glasteil ein grosses; ein fünfstöckiger Turm, ein dreistöckiger prismatischer Körper und der ein oder andere Körper, der über dem Glasteil herausragt.

1996. Lansondersingel, Enschede, The Netherlands.

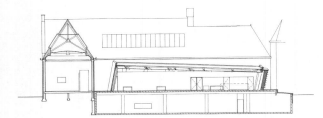

The old building of the National Museum of Twenthe is located in a very large block in the capital of this region, Enschede. It is slightly symetric with two greater sides and two lesser sides. The original building was built in 1928 and, taking advantage of the special geometry of the plot, it was projected as a set of parallel bodies in the adjacent streets, which enclosed a great central patio.

L'ancien bâtiment du Musée National de Twenthe se trouve dans un grand quartier de la capitale de cette région, Enschede. Sa forme est légèrement symétrique, avec deux côtés plus grands et deux plus petits. L'œuvre d'origine fut construite en 1928, et on utilisa la géométrie particulière du terrain. L'ouvrage fut organisé comme un ensemble de corps, parallèles aux rues attenantes, et clôturant une grande cour centrale.

Das alte Gebäude des Nationalmuseums von Twenthe befindet sich in einem großen Block in der Hauptstadt der Region, Enschede. Es hat eine leicht symetrische Form, mit zwei langen und zwei kurzen Seiten. Das ursprüngliche Gebäude wurde 1928 gebaut und profitiert von der Geometrie des Grundstücks: Die einzelnen Teile des Komplexes stehen parallel zu den angrenzenden Straßen rund um einen großen zentralen Innenhof.

The purpose of the small volume of glass and aluminum situated in the main patio is to connect the old museum route with the new. This piece was designed as a superposition with the old building.

Le petit volume de verre et d'aluminium situé dans la cour principale a pour but de relier le nouveau parcours muséographique à l'ancien. Cette pièce se présente comme une superposition à l'ancien édifice.

Der kleine Raum aus Glas und Aluminium im Haupthof dient zur Verbindung der neuen Ausstellungsräume mit den alten. Mit dem alten Gebäude wirkt dieses Stück wie eine Überblendung.

Mario **Botta**

The principal theme of all of Mario Botta's work is the recuperation of monumentality. His projects try to convoke a quality, often absent, from modern architecture that nonetheless was associated with this art for centuries.

Botta uses many of the architectural recourses of these types of construction. He uses simple and hermetic volumes and great masses covered with bricks or stone, that give no hint as to the interior.

Le thème principal de l'ensemble de l'œuvre de Mario Botta est la récupération de la monumentalité. Ses projets veulent réunir une qualité, souvent absente de l'architecture moderne, et qui a pourtant caractérisé cet art pendant des siècles.

Botta utilise de nombreuses ressources architectoniques de ce genre de constructions. Il utilise des volumes simples et hermétiques, de grande masses recouvertes de brique ou de pierre, qui ne fournissent aucune information sur l'intérieur du bâtiment.

Das Hauptthema des Gesamtwerkes von Mario Botta ist die Wiedergewinnung von Größe. Seine Projekte wollen eine häufig abwesende Qualität der modernen Architektur hervorrufen, die ohne Zweifel mit dieser Kunst jahrhundertelang verbunden war.

Botta nutzt viele der architektonischen Mittel dieses Bautyps. Er verwendet einfache und geschlossene Außenansichten, große Flächen, die mit Ziegeln oder Steinen verkleidet sind und keine Information über den Innenraum geben.

1943	Born in Mendrisio, Switzerland.	*Naît à Mendrisio, Suisse.*	geboren in Mendrisio, Schweiz.
1961-64	He studied at the *Liceo Artistico* in Milano.	*Etudie au* Liceo artistico *de Milan.*	Studium im *Liceo artistico* in Mailand.
1964-69	He studied at the *Instituto Universitario di Architettura di Venecia.*	*Etudie à l'*Istituto Universitario di Architettura di Venecia.	Studium im *Instituto Universitario di Architettura* in Venedig
1965	He worked in the Le Courbusier studio.	*Travaille à l'atelier de Le Courbusier.*	Arbeitet im Büro von Le Courbusier.
1969	He founded his own studio in Lugano.	*Fonde son agence à Lugano.*	Gründet sein eigenes Büro in Lugano.
1984	Honorary member of the *American Institute of Architects.*	*Membre honoraire de l'*American Institute of Architects.	Ehrenmitglied des *American Institute of Architects.*
1997	Honorary member of the *Royal Institute of British Architects.*	*Membre honoraire du* Royal Institute of British Architects.	Ehrenmitglied des *Royal Institue of British Architects.*
1999	*Chevalier dans l'Ordre national de la Legión d'Honneur in France.*	*Chevalier de l'Ordre national de la Légion d'Honneur, France.*	*Chevalier dans l´Ordre national de la Legion d´honneur in Frankreich.*

SAN FRANCISCO MUSEUM OF MODERN ART

1995. San Francisco, U.S.A.

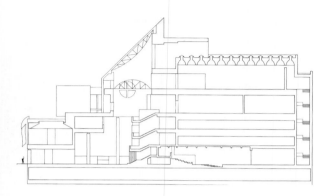

Botta employed symmetry as a method of organization, for the floor plan as well as for the exterior image of the building. The SFMOMA (the San Francisco Museum of Modern Art) is structured in clear axes following Beaux-Arts tradition. The architect defines the main facade, two laterals and a rear. The main facade is totally symmetrical and presents a volumetric hierarchy, whereby the height is the highest at the central point and gradually lowers as you go out to the edges. In spite of consisting of six floors, Botta illuminates the majority of the halls with natural zenithal light by means of a staggered design of the section.

Botta utilise la symétrie comme méthode d'organisation, tant du plan que de l'image extérieure du bâtiment. Le SFMOMA (San Francisco Museum of Modern Art) est structuré sur des axes nets selon la tradition Beaux-Arts. L'architecte définit une façade principale, deux latérales, et une arrière. La façade principale est strictement symétrique, et présente une hiérarchie volumétrique qui place le point central au plus haut, réduisant la hauteur vers les extrémités du bâtiment. En dépit des six étages de cette œuvre, Botta illumine la majorité des salles de lumière naturelle zénithale grâce à une conception échelonnée.

Botta nutzt die Symetrie sowohl in den Stockwerken als auch bei der äußeren Erscheinung des Gebäudes als Organisationsmethode. Das SFMOMA (San Francisco Museum of Modern Art) ist nach der Tradition der Beaux-Arts in klare Achsen strukturiert. Der Architekt definiert eine Haupt-, zwei seitliche und eine hintere Fassade. Die Hauptfassade ist komplett symetrisch und präsentiert eine räumliche Hierachie, in der die Höhe ihr Maximum im Zentrum erreicht und sich nach außen reduziert.Trotz der sechs Stockwerke beleuchtet Botta die meisten Säle durch ein abgestuftes Design mit natürlichem Licht.

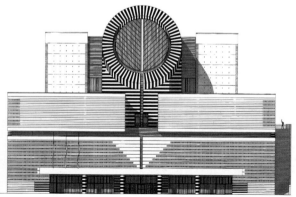

The density of the surroundings dictated the construction of a great central atrium, conceived as a great covered plaza.

La densité de l'emplacement a déterminé la construction d'un parvis central, conçu comme une grande place couverte.

Die Dichte der Umgebung bestimmt die Bauweise eines großen zentralen Innenhofs, der wie ein großer überdachter Platz begriffen werden kann.

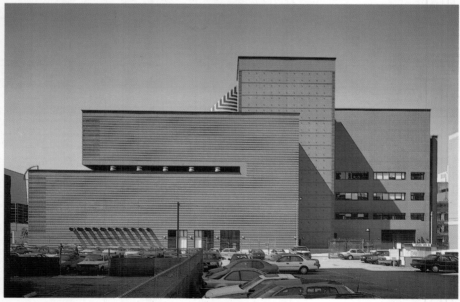

Botta takes advantage of the staggered nature of the building to place the halls only in the places where there is no floor above it.

Botta utilise l'échelonnement du bâtiment pour placer les salles uniquement dans les sections qui ne sont pas surmontées d'un étage.

Botta profitiert von der Staffelung des Gebäudes, um die Säle nur in den Streifen zu platzieren, in denen kein Stockwerk darüberliegt.

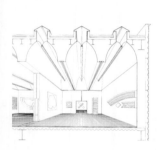

William P. **Bruder**

For the architect and scupturor William P. Bruder, architecture is a functional art based on the place and the needs of the user, and apart from having a clear practical objective, it must also be a poetic search. Bruder's works, acclimated to a desert setting where he developed the majority of his work, are an example of organic architecture and are characterized by the use of natural materials combined with blocks of concrete and sheets of metal.

Pour l'architecte et sculpteur William P. Bruder, l'architecture est un art fonctionnel basé sur le lieu et les nécessités de l'utilisateur. En plus de son objectif pratique clair, il doit constituer une quête poétique. Les réalisations de Bruder, acclimatées à l'environnement désertique qui est le décor de la majorité de ses œuvres, sont un exemple de l'architecture organique. Elles se caractérisent par l'utilisation de matériaux naturels, combinés à des blocs de béton et des plaques de métal.

Für den Architekten und Bildhauer William P. Bruder ist die Architektur eine funktionale Kunst, die auf dem Ort und den Bedürfnissen des Nutzers basiert und die außerdem ein klares praktisches Ziel hat. Sie muß auch eine poetische Suche sein. Die Werke von Bruder, die sich an die öde Umgebung anpassen, in der er die meisten seiner Arbeiten durchgeführt hat, sind ein Beispiel für organische Architektur und und zeichnen sich durch die Verwendung von natürlichen Materialien in Verbindung mit Betonblöcken und Metallplatten aus.

1946	He was born in Milwaukee, U.S.A.	*Naît à Milwaukee, Etats-Unis.*	Geboren in Milwaukee, USA.
1971	Professor at the *School of Architecture* at the *State University of Arizona.*	*Professeur à la* School of Architecture *de la* State University *d'Arizona.*	Dozent an der *School of Architecture* der *State University* von Arizona.
1974	He founded his own studio.	*Fonde son agence.*	Gründet sein eigenes Büro.
1977	*Record Home* Award.	*Prix* Record Home.	*Record Home*-Preis.
1987	*Rome* Award from the *American Academy* in Rome.	*Prix Rome de l'*American Academy in Rome.	*Roma*-Preis der *American Academy* in Rom.
1994	*Dupont Benedictus* Prize from the American Institute of Architects.	*Prix DuPont Benedictus de l'*American Institute of Architects.	*DuPont Benedictus*-Preis des *American Institute of Architects.*
1994	*Record Home* Award.	*Prix* Record Home.	*Record Home*-Preis.

TEMPLE KOL AMI

1994. Scottsdale, Arizona, U.S.A.

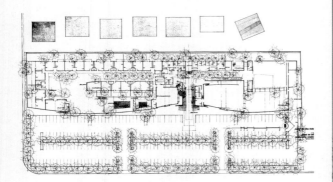

The project proposes the realization of a centrer of worship and learning in the form of an archaic town, with the spirit of the old Masada and Jerusalem communities. The architecture presents some Spartan spaces that acquire their definitive value from the precise entry of light, as much as for the physical reality as for the spiritual sense.

Le projet suggère la réalisation d'un centre de culte et d'apprentissage sous forme de village archaïque, dans l'esprit des anciennes communautés de Massada et Jérusalem. Son architecture dispose d'espaces spartiates qui n'acquièrent leur valeur définitive que par la percée précise de la lumière, tant par sa réalité physique que par sa signification spirituelle.

Das Projekt schlägt die Realisierung eines Kultur- und Lernzentrums in Form eines archaischen Dorfes mit dem Geist der alten Gemeinden von Masada und Jerusalem vor. Seine Architektur präsentiert einige spatanische Zwischenräume, die ihren definitiven Wert vom präzisen Lichteinfall ewerben, ebenso wie von ihrer physische Realität und ihrem spirituellen Sinn.

The use of concrete block achieves a special image. The irregular, dry surface convokes the image of millenarian, stone walls and transmits strong ties to the earth.

Le bloc de béton fournit une image singulière. Sa surface irrégulière et sèche évoque l'image des murs de pierre millénaires, et établit un lien fort avec la terre.

Die Nutzung von Betonblöcken schafft eine separates Bild. Die unregelmäßigentrockenen Oberflächen zeichnen ein Bild der tausendjährigen Steinmauern und übermitteln eine starke Verbindung mit der Erde.

RIDDELL'S

1995. Jackson Hole, Wyoming, U.S.A.

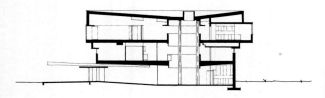

This three-storey office building has a central atrium as a nucleus: a vertical space illuminated by a long, narrow, rising window that when it reaches the ceiling, folds and transforms itself into a skylight. The wood is the tectonic theme of the project. It defines the dimension of the spaces while at the same time organizing the general lecture of the building.

Le cœur de cet ensemble de bureaux à trois étages est un parvis central: espace vertical illuminé par une fenêtre ascendante, étroite et élancée, qui se plie en rejoignant le toit pour former une lucarne. Le bois est le thème tectonique du projet; il articule la dimension des espaces et organise la lecture générale de l'ouvrage.

Dieses dreistöckige Bürogebäude hat einen zentrales Atrium im Mittelpunkt: ein vertikaler Raum, der durch ein aufsteigendes schmales langes Fenster beleuchtet wird, das sich bis unter das Dach einfügt und sich dann in eine Dachluke verwandelt. Das Holz ist das tektonische Thema des Projekts, es verbindet die Dimensionen der Räume miteinander, gleichzeitig ordnet es die allgemeine Sichtweise des Gebäudes.

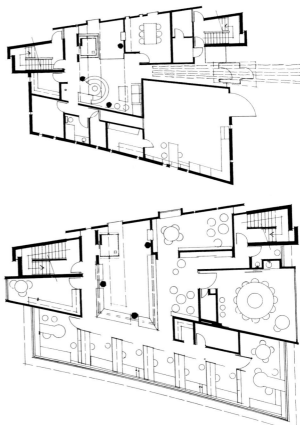

The walls are placed in perspective, dispersed, which makes the space dynamic, creating alterations that play with the perception of depth.

Les murs sont exposés en perspective, en fuite, ce qui dynamise l'espace et crée des altérations qui jouent avec la perspective de profondeur.

Die Mauern sind in perspektive gebaut, sie sind flüchtend, das macht den Raum dynamischer und schafft Veränderungen, die mit der Wahrnehmung der Tiefe spielen.

The roof of the two upper floors is guided, the width of the boards is regular which is different than the floor below and in the two stair towers.

Le bardage des deux étages supérieurs est maîtrisé, et la largeur des panneaux régulière, contrairement à celle de l'étage inférieur et des deux cages d'escalier.

Die Decke der zwei oberen Stockwerke ist geradlinig, die Breite der Bretter ist normal, im Gegensatz zu denen im unteren Stockwerk und denen in den zwei Treppenhäusern.

Santiago **Calatrava**

The design of the works of Santiago Calatrava is inspired in organic shapes very closely related to the parts of the body. With them he has replaced the rigid beams and pillars with more efficient elements that allow dynamic structures to be created by using traditional materials such as iron and concrete. Calatrava's architectural and engineering training have allowed him to balance art and functionality in works which are rarely completely closed structures.

Le design des œuvres de Santiago Calatrava s'inspire de formes organiques étroitement liées à des parties du corps humain. Les poutres et piliers rigides sont remplacés par des éléments plus efficaces qui permettent de créer des structures dynamiques, grâce à l'utilisation de matériaux traditionnels tels que le fer et le béton. La double formation de Calatrava en architecture et génie civil lui permit de conjuguer l'art et la fonctionnalité, dans des réalisations qui sont rarement des structures entièrement fermées.

Das Design der Werke von Santiago Calatrava ist von organischen Formen inspiriert, die eng mit dem menschlichen Körper verbunden sind. Mit ihnen ersetzt er starre Balken und Pfeiler durch wirksamere Elemente, die es erlauben, mit der Nutzung traditioneller Materialien wie Eisen und Beton, dynamische Strukturen zu schaffen. Die Ausbildung Calatravas zum Architekten und Ingenieur hat ihm erlaubt, Kunst und Funktionalität in Werken zu kombinieren, die seltsamerweise komplett geschlossenen Stukturen sind.

1951	Born in Valencia, Spain.	*Naît à Valence, Espagne.*	Geboren in Valencia, Spanien.
1969-74	He studied at the *Escuela Superior de Arquitectura* in Valencia.	*Etudie à l'*Escuela Técnica Superior de Arquitectura *de Valence.*	Studium an der *Escuela Técnica Superior de Arquitectura* in Valencia.
1975-81	He studied at the *Eidgenössische Technische Hochshule* in Zurich.	*Etudie à l'*Eidgenössische Technische Hochshule *de Zurich.*	Studium an der *Eidgenössischen Technischen Hochschule* (Zürich).
1981	He founded his own studio in Zurich.	*Fonde son agence à Zurich.*	Gründet sein eigenes Büro in Zürich.
1993	Honorary member of the *Royal Institute of British Architects.*	*Membre honoraire du* Royal Institute of British Architects.	Ehrenmitglied des *Royal Institute of Brisitsh Architects.*
1995	Fine Arts Gold Medal of Merit from the Government of Spain.	*Médaille d'Or du Mérite des Beaux-Arts (Gouvernement espagnol).*	*Medalla de Oro al Mérito de las Bellas Artes der spanischen Regierung.*
1995	European Award for Steel Structures.	European Award for Steel Structures.	*European Award for Steel Structures*
1999	Prince of Asturias for the Arts Award, Oviedo, Spain.	*Prix du Prince des Asturies pour l'Art, Oviedo, Espagne.*	*Premio Príncipe de Asturias de las Artes,* Oviedo, Spanien

Gare TGV Lyon-Satôlas

1996. Lyon, France.

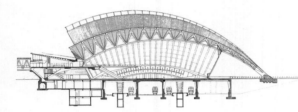

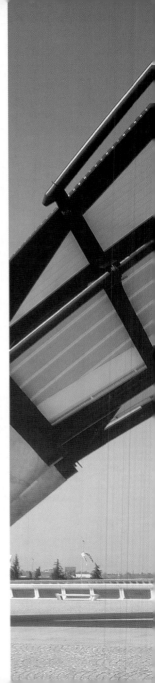

"My work is more figurative than organicist, in the sense that what interests me are certain sculptural-anatomical associations, always based on tremendously purist, static models. If you work with isostatic structures, it almost always inevitable brings you to schemes of nature". In the Lyon-Satôlas train station, Calatrava uses his two favorite composition mechanisms: symmetry and duality.

"Mon travail se veut plus figuratif qu'organiciste, en cela que je me concentre sur des associations précises sculpture-anatomie, toujours basées sur des modèles statiques extrêmement puristes. Travailler avec des structures isostatiques mène inévitablement à des schémas de la nature". Pour la gare de Lyon-Satolas, Calatrava utilise ses deux procédés de composition favoris: la symétrie et la dualité.

"Meine Arbeit ist mehr darstellend als organisch, das heißt, was mich interessiert sind bestimmte bildhauerische-anatomische Verbindungen, die immer auf schrecklich puristischen statischen Modellen basieren. Mit isostatischen Strukturen arbeiten bringt dich fast unausweichlich zu Schemen aus der Natur". Im Bahnhof Lyon-Satôlas hat Cataltrava seine beiden bevorzugt kombinierten Mechanismen benutzt: Symetrie und Dualität.

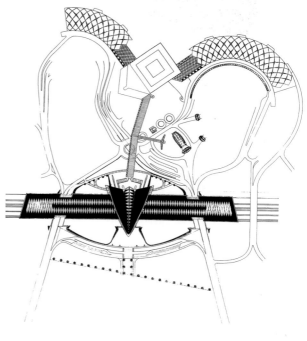

Like in the majority of Calatrava projects, the materials are reduced almost exclusively to three: concrete, steel and glass. Surely, one of the reasons is the importance of structure in the final appearance of the building. There are hardly any coverings nor partitions.

Comme pour la majorité des réalisations de Calatrava, les matériaux sont réduits presque exclusivement au béton, à l'acier et au verre. Ce choix peut sûrement s'expliquer par l'importance de la structure dans l'aspect final du bâtiment. Les revêtements et partitions sont quasi absents.

Wie in den meisten Projekten Calatravas reduzieren sich die Materialien fast ausschließlich auf drei: Beton, Stahl und Glas. Einer der Gründe ist sicher die Bedeutung der Struktur in der Endansicht des Gebäudes. Es gibt kaum Verkleidungen oder Aufteilungen.

The Lyon-Satôlas train station is the first that connects an airport with a high-speed rail network in Europe.

La gare de Lyon-Satolas est la première en Europe à réunir un aéroport et une gare TGV.

Der Bahnhof Lyon-Satôlas ist der erste in Europa, der einen Flughafen mit einem Hochgeschwindigkeits-Schienennetz vereint.

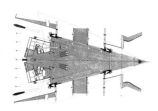

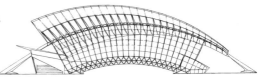

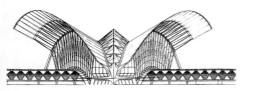

The covering of the vestibule is the emblematical element of the station. Two giant, steel arches are supported at the vertex of the triangle situated at the entrance and at the two vertexes of the opposite side, delimiting the north and south facades.

La toiture du hall est un élément emblématique de la gare. Deux gigantesques arcs d'acier reposent sur le sommet du triangle situé face à l'entrée, et sur les sommets des côtés opposés, définissant les façades nord et sud.

Das Dach der Vorhalle ist das emblematiche Element des Bahnhofs. Zwei gigantische Stahlbögen stützen sich an den Scheitelpunkten des Dreiecks neben dem Eingang und an dem gegenüberliegenden Ende, das die Nord- und Südfassade definieret.

Coop **Himmelb(l)au**

The Coop Himmelb(l)au does not understand architecture without fantasy. It is ground-breaking, hard and unsettling, too strange to be classified. From their beginnings, Wolf D. Prix and Helmut Swiczinsky were determined to explore new forms of construction in order to offer radical proposals that break with existing concepts and disturb the spectator, like their inflatable architecture projects or those which are inspired in the changing nature of the clouds.

L'équipe de Coop Himmelb(l)au ne conçoit pas l'architecture sans fantaisie. Son langage se veut rupturiste, dur et inconfortable, assez étrange pour être inclassable. Dès leurs débuts, Wolf D. Prix et Helmut Swiczinsky ont voulu explorer de nouvelles formes de construction pour offrir des réalisations radicales, rompant ainsi avec les concepts existants, et déconcertant le spectateur. C'est le cas de leurs projets d'architecture gonflable ou de ceux qui s'inspirent de la nature changeante des nuages.

Das Team von Coop Himmelb(l)au versteht die Architektur nich ohne Fantasie. Ihre Sprache ist gebrochen, schwer und unbequem, zu sonderbar um klassifiziert werden zu können. Von Beginn an haben Wolf D. Prix und Helmut Swicywinskz sich vorgenommen neue Bauformen zu erkunden, um radikale Vorschläge anzubieten, die mit den existierenden Konzepten brechen und den Betrachter stören, wie ihre übertriebenen architektonischen Projekte, oder die, die sich von der wechselhaften Natur der Wolken inspirieren lassen.

	Wolf D Prix was born in Viena, Austria, in 1942. Helmut Swiczinsky was born in Poznan, Poland, in 1944.	*Wolf D. Prix naît à Vienne, Autriche, en 1942. Helmut Swiczinsky naît à Poznan, Pologne, en 1944.*	Wolf D. Prix ist 1942 in Wien, Österreich, geboren. Helmut Swicyinsky ist 1944 ist Posen, Polen, geboren.
	They studied in the *Technische Universität Wien* y in the *Architectural Association School* in London. Prix also studied in the *California Institute of Architecture*.	*Ils étudient à la* Technische Université Wien *et à l'*Architectural Association School *de Londres.* Wolf D. Prix *étudie également au* Southern California Institute of Architecture.	Sie haben an der Technischen Universität Wien und der Architectural Association School in London studiert. Prix hat auch am Southern California Institute of Architecture studiert.
1968	Prix and Swiczinsky founded Coop Himmelb(l)au, in Viena.	*W. D. Prix et H. Swiczinsky fondent Coop Himmelb(l)au, à Vienne.*	Prix und Swiczinsky gründen Coop Himmelb(l)au in Wien
1988	Their studio opened a second office in Los Angeles, California.	*L'agence ouvre une filiale à Los Angeles, Californie.*	Das Büro eröffnet eine Filiale in Los Angeles, Kalifornien
1992	Erich Schelling Award.	*Prix Erich Schelling.*	Erich-Schelling-Preis
1999	*Deutscher Architekturpreis.*	Deutscher Architekturpreis.	Deutscher Architekturpreis

FORSCHUNGSZENTRUM SEIBERSDORF

1995. Seibersdorf, Österreich.

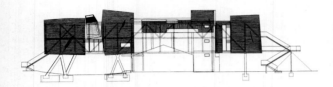

The project can be understood as a variation on the themes of beam, space and interior. Beam is the new building; space and interior the concepts questioned in the sense that they are not static, closed and defined, contrary to what would be exterior.
The commission consisted of the renovation and enlargement of an existing warehouse on the grounds of the Seibersdorf Research Center. The warehouse had to be modified and enlarged in such a way that the offices of the Center could be installed there.

Le projet peut être vu comme une variation sur les thèmes poutre, espace et intérieur. La poutre est le bâtiment nouveau; l'espace et l'intérieur, deux concepts remis en question. En effet, ils ne sont pas statiques, fermés et définis, par opposition avec ce qui leur serait extérieur. Il s'agissait d'un projet de réforme et d'extension d'un entrepôt existant sur les terrains du Centre de recherche Seibersdorf. L'entrepôt devait être modifié et élargi, de manière à pouvoir accueillir les bureaux du centre.

Das Projekt kann als eine als eine Variation von Balken, Platz und Innenraum verstanden werden. Balken ist das neue Gebäude; Platz und Innenraum, die Konzepte in Frage gestellt, sinngemäß sind sie nicht etwas statisches, geschlossenes und definiertes, dem entgegengesetzt, was aussen wäre. Der Auftrag bestand in der Reform und Vergrößerung eines existierenden Lagers auf dem Gelände des Forschungszentrums Seibersdorf. Das Lager mußte modifiziert und vergrößert werden, so daß es die Büros des Forschungszentrums aufnehmen konnte.

Christian **Drevet**

LE SÉMAPHORE

This French architect projected in his native country unusual public works such as auditoriums, schools, libraries, gymnasiums or funeral buildings on which he stamped his own personality with original and suggestive designs. He used nature and everyday objects as the source of his inspiration to give life to his proposals. Thus, elements such as a rainbow, a rug or a traffic light are changed into a facade, a ceiling or an indication of his constructions.

Cet architecte français a conçu dans son pays natal des bâtiments publics singuliers (auditoriums, écoles, bibliothèques, gymnases, monuments funéraires), auxquels il a donné une personnalité propre par des designs originaux et suggestifs. Pour donner de la vie à ses œuvres, il s'inspire de la nature et d'objets de la vie quotidienne. Ainsi, des éléments tels qu'un arc-en-ciel, un tapis ou un feu de signalisation deviennent une façade, une toiture ou un panneau indicateur de ses œuvres.

Dieser französische Architekt hat in seinem Heimatland einzelne öffentliche Werke entworfen, wie z.B. Auditorien, Schulen, Bibliotheken, Sporthallen oder Bestattungsgebäude, denen er eine eigene Persönlichkeit durch originelle und anregende Designs gebeben hat. Die Inspiration, mit der er seine Projekte ins Leben ruft, hat er in der Natur und in Alltagsgegenständen gefunden. So verwandeln sich Elemente wie der Regenbogen, ein Teppich oder eine Ampel in eine Fassade, ein Dach, oder eine Anzeigetafel in seinen Bauwerken.

1951	He was born in Lyon, France.	*Naît à Lyon, France.*	Geboren in Lyon, Frankreich.
1980	He obtained his architecture degree and began to work free-lance.	*Obtient le diplôme d'architecte et devient travailleur autonome.*	Erhält den Titel Architekt und beginnt als Selbstständiger seine Arbeit.
1980-91	Professor at the *École d'Architecture de Lyon*.	*Professeur à l'École d'architecture de Lyon.*	Dozent an der *École d'architecture* in Lyon.
1982-90	Urban consultant at the *Conseil d'Architecture, d'Urbanisme et de l'Environnement du Rhône*.	*Consultant auprès du Conseil d'Architecture, d'Urbanisme et de l'Environnement du Rhône.*	Beratender Stadtplaner *im Conseil d'Architecture, d'Urbanisme et de l'Environnement du Rhône*.
1990-94	Urban consultant in the *Conseil du Grand Lyon*.	*Urbaniste consultant auprès du Conseil du Grand Lyon.*	Stadtrat für Stadtplanung im *Conseil du Grand Lyon*.
1992	Consultant architect in the *Mission Interministérielle pour la Qualité des Constructions Publiques*.	*Architecte consultant auprès de la Mission Interministérielle pour la Qualité des Constructions Publiques.*	Beratender Architekt in der *Mission Interministérielle pour la Qualité des Constructions Publiques*.
1994	Professor at the *École d'Architecture de Saint-Étienne*.	*Professeur à l'École d'architecture de Saint-Étienne.*	Dozent an der *École d'architecture de Saint-Étienne*.

LE SÉMAPHORE

1994. Roussillon, France.

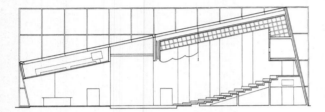

Le Sémaphore is a multi-use performance hall. The project plays with three elements: a luminous mast, a metal screen and a parallelepiped which are fitted into the landscape according to the parameters of the structuralist philosophy: point, line and plane. The slant of the roof of the box is determined by the high height which the different functions of the interior spaces demand.

Le Sémaphore est une salle polyvalente dont la réalisation repose sur trois éléments: un mât lumineux, un écran métallique et un parallélépipède. Tous trois s'inscrivent dans le paysage selon les paramètres de la philosophie structuraliste: point, ligne et plan. L'inclinaison de la toiture du bâtiment est déterminée par les exigences de hauteur des espaces intérieurs pour leurs différentes fonctions.

Le Sémaphore ist ein Mehrzwecksaal, dessen Entwurf mit drei Elementen spielt: ein erleuchteter Mast, eine Metallleinwand und ein Parallelepipedon, die sich nach den Parametern der Strukturphilosophie in die Landschaft einfügen: punktuell, gerade und flach. Die Neigung des Daches des Kastens wird von der Höhe bestimmt, die für die verschiedenen Funktionen der Innenräune erforderlich ist.

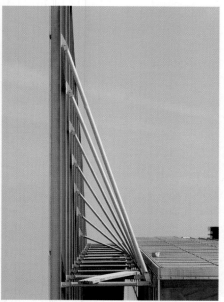

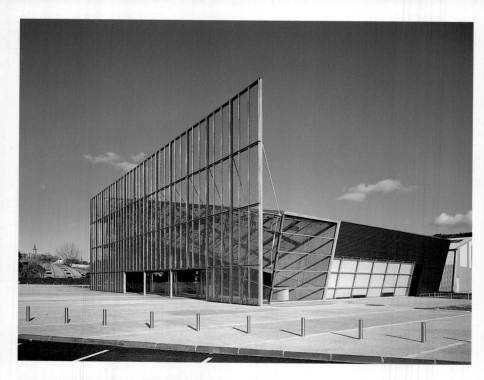

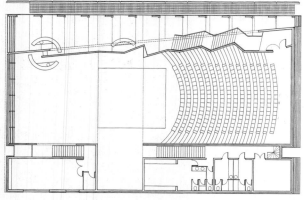

The metal screen of the facade evokes a stage scene. Behind it there is a second skin of glass and behind this, a wall which folds like a curtain.

L'écran métallique de la façade évoque un tableau scénique. Derrière l'écran se trouve une deuxième couche de verre, puis un mur qui se plie comme un rideau.

Die Metallfläche der Fassade verhindert einen szenischen Anblick. Hinter ihr gibt es eine zweite Haut aus Glas und, dahinter, eine Mauer, die sich wie eine Gardine einfügt.

Le Sémaphore is situated in a great public place. The building is like a great event within the plaza, which invites you to look in, to what is happening inside.

Le Sémaphore s'inscrit dans un grand espace public. Le bâtiment est comme un grand événement sur la place, une invitation à rentrer pour voir ce qui s'y passe.

Le Sémaphore fügt sich in einen großen öffenttlichen Raum ein. Das Gebäude ist wie ein großes Ereignis mitten auf dem Platz, das dazu einlädt nachzuschauen, was drinnen passiert.

Erick **Van Egeraat**

Eric Van Egeraat began in his student period with a few surprising proposals within an architectural tradition of forceful and simple ideas. Nevertheless, in his professional development his concepts have progressively become enriched and directed at cultural mixes, or even the fusion of architecture with fashion. Considering his buildings as inclusion, his projects are seen as more daring and his proposals are more and more striking and innovative all the time.

Pendant ses études, Eric Van Egeraat réalise des projets qui s'inscrivent dans une tradition architectonique d'idées percutantes et simples. Cependant, ses concepts vont s'enrichir au fil de sa carrière professionnelle, et se diriger vers des mélanges culturels, allant jusqu'à la fusion de l'architecture et de la mode. Envisageant ses ouvrages comme inclusion, ses réalisations se révèlent chaque fois plus audacieuses, tranchantes et innovatrices.

Eric Van Egeraat hat in seiner Epoche als Student mit Vorschlägen begonnen, die sich in eine schlagkräftige und schlichte architektonische Tradition eingefügt haben. Trotzdem waren seine Konzepte in seiner beruflichen Entwicklung berreichernd und haben sich zur Mischung der Kulturen bewegt, oder auch zur Fusion seiner Architektur mit der Mode. Betrachtet man seine Gebäude als Einschluß, präsentieren sich seine Projekte viel dreister jedes Mal mit gegensätzlicheren und innovativeren Vorschlägen.

1956	He was born in Amsterdam, The Netherlands.	*Naît à Amsterdam, Pays-Bas.*	Geboren in Amsterdam, Niederlande.
1984	He graduated from the *Technical University* of Delft.	*Diplômé de la* Technical University *de Delft.*	Abschluß an der *Technical University* von Delft.
1984	Co-founder of *Mecanoo Architekten.*	*Cofondateur de* Mecanoo Architekten.	Mitbegründer von *Mecanoo Architekten.*
1995	He founded *Erick Van Egeraat Associated Architects,* in Rotterdam and Budapest.	*Fonde* Erick Van Egeraat Associated Architects, *à Rotterdam et Budapest.*	Gründet *Eric Van Egeraat Associated Architects* in Rotterdam und Budapest.
1996	Honorary member of the *Bund Deutshcer Architekten.*	*Membre honoraire du* Bund Deutscher Architekten.	Ehrenmitglied des *Bundes Deutscher Architekten.*
1998	He opened an office of his studio in London.	*Ouvre une filiale de son agence à Londres.*	Eröffnet ein weiteres Büro in London.
1999	He opened an office in Prague.	*Ouvre une autre filiale à Prague.*	Eröffnet einen Büro in Prag.
2001	Honorary member of the *Royal Institute of British Architects.*	*Membre honoraire du* Royal Institute of British Architects.	Ehrenmitglied des *Royal Institute of British Architects.*

1997. Utrecht, The Netherlands.

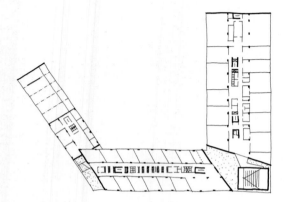

When the "eea" team was contacted to undertake this project, the building had already been projected by another architect. That is to say, they didn't charge him with the building of a new construction but rather they asked him to intervene in a project already started in order to obtain the approval of the "aesthetic" Committee of the region. The main objective of the commission was to revitalize the image of the building already projected by another architect, and of a secondary nature, to rethink the access to the vestibule.

Lorsque l'équipe "eea" fut contactée pour réaliser ce projet, un plan avait déjà été établi par un autre architecte. Il ne s'agissait donc pas d'élaborer un nouveau plan, mais d'intervenir sur un projet déjà existant, dans le but d'obtenir l'aval du Comité "esthétique" de la région. La mission principale était de revitaliser l'image du bâtiment élaboré par l'autre architecte, et dans un deuxième temps, de remodeler le hall d'entrée.

Als das Team "eea" wurde er zur Realisierung dieses Projektes kontaktiert, das Gebäude war schon von einem anderen Achitekten entworfen worden.Das heißt, er hat nichtdie Planung eines neuen Gebäudes übernommen, sondern man hat ihn gebeten, in ein bereits bestehendes Projekt einzugreifen, mit dem Ziel, die Zustimmung des "Ästhetik"-Komitees der Region zu bekommen. Das Hauptziel des Zuständigen war die Belebung der Erscheinung des Gebäudes, das schon von einem anderen Architekten entworfen worden war, und sekundär, die Vorhalle zu überarbeiten.

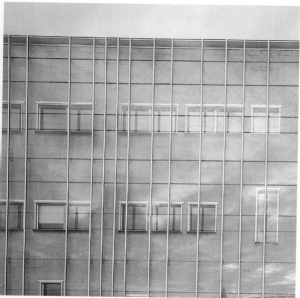

The architects opt for designing a glass skin which is superimposed in a completely independent way on the already existing facade. Thus the building turns out to be enveloped in a kind of veil which reveals but at the same time transforms.

Les architectes choisissent d'ajouter une couche de verre, qui se superpose à la façade existante de manière complètement indépendante. Le bâtiment est ainsi enveloppé dans une sorte de voile, qui à la fois laisse paraître et transforme.

Die Architekten haben sich entschieden, die Außenseite mit Glas zu verkleiden, das sich komplett unabhängig auf die bereits existierende Fassade legt. So bleibt das Gebäude mit einer Art Schleier verhüllt, der zeigt, aber gleichzeitig auch verändert.

NATURE MUSEUM. ROTTERDAM

1995. Rotterdam, The Netherlands.

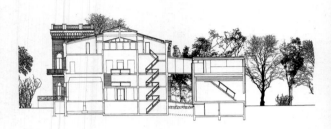

This museum is situated in the "Park of the Museums" in the city of Rotterdam. Taking advantage of a restoration iniciative of the old town, it was decided that an annex would be built which would enable the museum to be enlarged. The new building holds a great hall for temporary exhibitions on the ground floor and the offices and a library on the first floor. From Villa Dijkzigt you have access to the annex by means of a covered catwalk which sets out from the entrance of the building. Both constructions are separated by an elongated Japanese garden of Japanese inspiration. The facade is conceived, according to Van Egeraat, as the sum of three distinct skins.

Ce musée se trouve dans le "Parc des Musées" de la ville de Rotterdam. Profitant de la restauration de la vieille ville, une annexe fut construite pour agrandir le musée. Le nouveau bâtiment héberge une grande salle d'expositions temporaires au rez-de-chaussée, et des bureaux, ainsi que la bibliothèque, au premier étage. L'accès à l'annexe se fait depuis Villa Dijkzigt par une passerelle couverte qui part de l'entrée du bâtiment. Les deux constructions sont séparées par un jardin étendu d'inspiration japonaise. Selon Van Egeraat, la façade est conçue comme la somme de trois couches distinctes.

Dieses Museum befindet sich im "Park der Museen" in Rotterdam. Eine Initiative zur Restaurierung der alten Villa nutzend, hat man sich entschieden, einen Anbau zu machen, der das Museum vergrößert. Das neue Gebäude beherbergt im Erdgeschoß einen großen Saal für temporäre Ausstellungen und Büros und die Bibliothek im ersten Stock. Von der Villa Dijkzigt aus betritt man den Anbau über einen überdachten Durchgang, der vom Eingang des Gebäudes ausgeht. Beide Konstruktionen sind durch einen verlängerten Garten mit japanischem Einfluß getvennt. Die Fassade muß laut Van Egeraat als eine Summe aus drei Verkleidungen begriffen werden.

A great sliding window, with fixed glass, without a frame, and at floor level, illuminates the temporary exhibition hall in such a way that you can only see the grass that surrounds the building.

Une longue baie aux vitres fixes, sans charpente, et au niveau du sol, illumine la salle d'expositions temporaires et ne laisse paraître que la pelouse entourant le bâtiment.

Ein großes verschobenes Fenster mit festem Glas, ohne Holz und auf der Höhe des Bodens bringt Licht in den Austellungssaal, so daß man nur einen einzigen Blick auf den Rasen hat, der rundum das Gebäude angelegt ist.

If you arrive at the museum from the park, the first image is dominated by the annex to the vestibule: a whale suspended in the air is outlined by a concrete wall behind it, as if it was enclosed in a giant fishbowl in the middle of the forest.

Si l'on accède au musée par le parc, la première image est celle du hall de l'annexe: une baleine suspendue se découpe sur un mur en béton, comme enfermée dans un aquarium géant au milieu du bois.

Wenn man vom Park aus zum Museum kommt, wird der erste Eindruck von der Vorhalle des Anbaus dominiert: Eine Stange, die in der Luft endet hebt sich gegen eine Betonwand als wäre sie in einem riesigen Aquarium mitten im Wald eingesperrt.

Lord Norman **Foster**

Although the first works of Norman Foster are austere, his work has evolved with the utilization of curved surfaces and the adoption of new construction materials. This experimentation process allowed him to play with shapes until he created his own recognizable style within the "high tech" movement, with structures that look like metal skeletons covered with light, translucent layers and organic designs that demostrate his mastery of technique.

En dépit de l'austérité des premières œuvres de Norman Foster, ses réalisations ont évoluées avec l'utilisation de surfaces courbes et l'adoption de nouveaux matériaux de construction. Ce processus d'expérimentation lui a permis de jouer avec les formes, jusqu'à créer un style propre et identifiable au sein du courant "High Tech". Les structures semblables à des squelettes métalliques recouverts de légères couches translucides, et les formes organiques, témoignent d'une haute maîtrise de la technique.

Auch wenn die ersten Werke von Norman Foster karg sind, hat sich seine Arbeit mit dem Gebrauch von runden Oberflächen und der Verwendung neuer Baumaterialien entwickelt.Ein experimenteller Prozess, der ihm erlaubt hat mit den Formen zu spielen, bis er einen eigenen Stil entwickelt hat, der im "High Tech"-Strom wiedererkennbar ist, mit Strukturen, die aussehen wie Metallskelette, bedeckt mit leichten lichtdurchlässigen Schichten und organischen Designs, die eine große Dominaz der Technik zeigen.

1935	Born in Manchester, The United Kingdom.	Naît à Manchester, Royaume-Uni.	Geboren in Manchester, Grossbritannien
1961	Graduated from the *School of Architecture and City Planning* of the University of Manchester and wins a scholarship to The University of Yale, where he obtains a master in architecture.	Obtient le diplôme de la School of Architecture and City Planning *de l'Université de Manchester, et décroche une bourse pour l'Université de Yale, où il obtient un Master en architecture.*	Abschluß in der *School of Architecture and City Planning* der Universität Manchester und er bekam ein Stipendium für die Universität von Yale, wo er ein Master in Architektur gemacht hat.
1963	Co-founder with Richard Rogers of *Team 4* studio.	Cofondateur, avec Richard Rogers, de l'agence Team 4.	Mitbegründer des Büros *Team 4* mit Richard Rogers
1967	Founds *Foster Associates*, now *Foster and Partners*.	Fonde Foster Associates, aujourd'hui Foster and Partners.	Gründet *Foster Associates*, heute *Foster and Partners*.
1983	Gold Medal from the *Royal Institute of British Architects*.	Médaille d'Or du Royal Institute of British Architects.	Goldmedallie des *Royal Institute of British Architects*.
1991	Gold Medal from the *L'Académie FranÇaise d'Architecture*.	Médaille d'Or de l'Académie Française d'Architecture.	Goldmedallie der *Académie Française d'Architecture*.
1999	Pritzker Prize of Architecture.	Prix Pritzker d'Architecture.	Pritzker-Preis für Architektur.

COMMERZBANK

1997. Frankfurt, Deutschland.

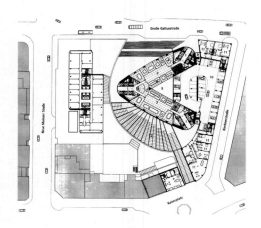

This is the most important project undertaken by the city of Frankfurt in the last few decades and constitutes the first example of a skyscraper designed under ecological criteria. Each office is designed to have natural ventilation by means of movable/openable windows which also enable you to enjoy the views of the city and the great patios with gardens. The plot shares the block with other blocks of flats that occupy the southeast corner, and the tower of the old headquarters of the Commerzbank.

C'est le plus important projet entrepris par la ville de Frankfort depuis ces dernières décennies. Il est le premier exemple de gratte-ciel élaboré à partir de critères écologiques. Chaque bureau est conçu de façon à obtenir une ventilation naturelle grâce aux fenêtres ouvrantes, et à jouir d'une vue sur la ville et sur les espaces verts. Près du bâtiment se trouvent la tour de l'ancien siège de la Commerzbank, et côté sud-ouest, des immeubles d'habitations.

Dieses Projekt ist das wichtigste, das von der Stadt Frankfurt am Main in den letzten Dekaden angeschnitten wurde. Es konstituiert das erste Beispiel eines Wolkenkratzers, der nach ökologischen Kriterien entworfen wurde. Jedes Büro ist so geplant, daß es eine natürliche Belüftung über praktische Fenster hat und daß man einen Blick über die Stadt und begrünte Innenhöfe hat. Das Grundstück teilt sich den Block mit anderen Wohnhäusern und dem Turm des ehemaligen Sitzes der Commerzbank, die im Südwesten stehen.

The relationship of the buildings with the surroundings is of great importance. The triangle-shaped tower is aesthetically combined with the buildings that already exist as well as with the new block of apartments.

Le lien avec les bâtiments voisins est de grande importance. La tour triangulaire s'appuie autant sur les constructions existantes que sur le nouveau bloc d'appartements.

Die Beziehung zwischen den Gebäuden und der Umgebung ist sehr wichtig. Der dreickige Turm kombiniert sich genauso mit den existierenden Gebäuden, wie der neue Apartementblock.

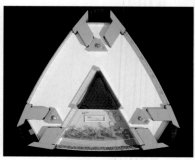

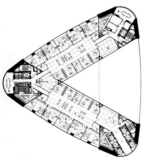

Only from the main entrance in the north, the tower appears before us with all of its majestic height from ground level.

Seul l'accès principal nord nous laisse mesurer la hauteur majestueuse de la tour depuis la cote du sol.

Nur vom Haupteingang im Norden erscheint der Turm in seiner gesamten majestetischen Höhe vom Boden an.

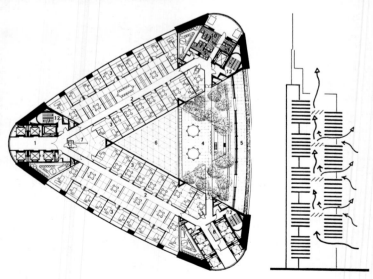

Faculty of Law, University of Cambridge

1995. Cambridge Campus, United Kingdom.

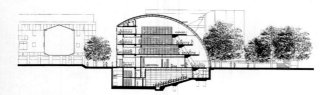

The new faculty includes five auditoriums, seminars, meeting rooms, administration and a large library totaling 9,000 square meters which occupy six floors, two of which are underground thereby interfering as little as possible with the present silhouette of the campus. The basement floor has classrooms for diverse uses, administration and other spaces for the personnel. The basement floors are occupied with three large auditoriums, deposits for books and meeting rooms for students whereas the last three top floors are reserved for the library.

La nouvelle faculté s'étend sur 9.000 m², et comprend cinq auditoriums, des séminaires, des salles de réunion, une administration et une grande bibliothèque. Deux des six étages sont sous-terre, de manière à interférer le moins possible avec le profil actuel du campus. Au rez-de-chaussée se trouvent des salles d'usages divers, l'administration, et autres espaces pour le personnel. Les étages souterrains sont occupés par trois grands auditoriums, les archives, et des salles de réunion pour les étudiants. Les trois étages supérieurs sont réservés à la bibliothèque.

Die neue Fakulktät hat fünf Hörsäle, Seminarräume, Konferenzsäle, Verwaltung und eine große Bibliothek, insgesamt 9000 m² auf 6 Etagen von denen zwei unter der Erde sind, so, daß sie im aktuellen Gesamtbild des Campus so wenig wie möglich in Erscheinung tritt. Das Erdgeschoß hat Mehrzweckräume, Verwaltung und andere Räume für das Personal.

The basement floors are occupied with three large auditoriums, deposits for books and meeting rooms for students whereas the last three top floors are reserved for the library.

Les étages souterrains sont occupés par trois grands auditoriums, les archives, et des salles de réunion pour les étudiants. Les trois étages supérieurs sont réservés à la bibliothèque.

Die Kellergeschosse haben drei grosse Hörsäle, Buchläden und Aufenthaltsräume für die Studenten, während die drei oberen Etagen der Bibliothek vorbehalten sind.

The use of technology enables the construction of a glassed membrane which envelopes the building allowing the introduction of natural light within the spaces.

L'utilisation de la technologie permet la construction d'une membrane de verre, qui enveloppe le bâtiment et laisse la lumière naturelle envahir l'espace intérieur.

Die Nutzung der Technologie erlaubt die Konstruktion einer Kristallmembran, die das Gebäude einpackt, und dem Tageslicht die Möglichkeit gibt, durch diesselbe einzudringen.

Haus in Deutschland

1994. Luedenscheid, Deutschland.

The present case means the adaptation to domestic premises of Foster's concern for human necessities and the appropriate use of technique to resolve it. Also, the sensitiveness to integrate and relate the house with the landscape. This is demonstrated by a section which recognizes the profile of the terrain and in the exterior orientation of all of the rooms of the dwelling.

Ce projet illustre l'adaptation à des prémisses domestiques du soucis de Foster pour les besoins de l'homme, et pour l'utilisation correcte de la technique pour les résoudre. Il reflète également le désir d'intégrer et de relier la maison au paysage, qui se traduit par une section qui reconnaît le profil du terrain, et par l'orientation extérieure de toutes les pièces de la maison.

Der aktuelle Fall geht von einer Anpassung an einige häusliche Vorraussetzungen von Fosters Sorge für die menschlichen Bedürfnisse und die adäquate Anwendung der Technik um diese zu lösen aus, ebenso wie von der Sensibilität zur Integration und Verbindung des Hauses mit der Landschaft, was sich in einer Sektion übersetzt, die das Profil des Geländes anerkennt und die äußere Orientierung aller Wohnräume des Wohnhauses anerkennt.

The program of the dwelling is developed in two floors which are connected and with the access level by means of an interior ramp that runs parallel to the contention wall.

La maison comprend deux étages, qui communiquent par une rampe intérieure parallèle au mur de retenue.

Das Programm des Wohnhauses verläuft auf zwei Etagen, die mit einem Zugang über eine Rampe, die parallel zur Stützmauer verläuft, verbunden sind.

Frank O. **Gehry**

The works of the architect and designer Frank O. Gehry have a certain deconstructivist aesthetic to them and they are characterized by the juxtaposition of simple geometric shapes that are designed as true sculptural objects. Gehry has investigated the expressive potential of materials such as plywood, metal or concrete to carry out works that are far from conventionalisms, and apart from being spectacular, seem to enjoy having an unfinished appearance.

Les œuvres de l'architecte-designer Frank O. Gehry obéissent à une certaine esthétique déconstructiviste, et se caractérisent par une juxtaposition de formes géométriques simples, élaborées comme de véritables objets sculpturaux. Gehry a exploré le potentiel expressif de matériaux tels que le bois contreplaqué, le métal ou le béton, pour réaliser des œuvres qui s'éloignent du conventionnalisme, et qui, en plus d'être spectaculaires, semblent se complaire dans leur aspect d'œuvres inachevées.

Die Arbeiten des Architekten und Designers Frank O. Gehry haben eine bestimmte destruktive Ästhetik und zeichnen sich durch die Juxtaposition der einfachen geometrischen Formen aus, die wie richtige bildhauerische Objekte entworfen worden sind. Gehry hat das ausdrucksvolle Potential der Materialien, wie furniertes Holz, Metal oder Beton erforscht, um Arbeiten durchzuführen, die sich vom Konventialismus entfernen, und die außer das sie spektakulär sind, sich scheinbar mit ihrer unvollendeten Erscheinung zufrieden geben.

1929	Born in Toronto, Canada.	*Naît à Toronto, Canada.*	Geboren in Toronto, Kanada.
1954	Architecture degree from the *University of Southern California.*	*Diplôme d'architecte de l'*University of Southern California.	Titel in Architektur an der *University of Southern California.*
1956-57	Urban planning studies in the *Graduate School of Design* at the University of Harvard.	*Etudes de planification urbaine de la* Graduate School of Design *de l'Université de Harvard.*	Studium der Stadtplanung an der *Graduate School of Design* der Havard-Universität.
1962	Found his first studio, *Frank O. Gehry and Associates.*	*Fonde sa première agence,* Frank O. Gehry and Associates.	Gründet sein erstes Büro, *Frank O. Gehry and Associates.*
1974	Member of the *College of Fellows, American Institute of Architects.*	*Membre du* College of Fellows, American Institute of Architects.	Mitglied des *College of Fellows, American Institute of Architects.*
1979	Founds *Gehry & Krueger Inc.*	*Fonde* Gehry & Krueger Inc.	Gründet *Gehry & Krueger Inc.*
1989	Pritzker Award of Architecture.	*Prix Pritzker d'Architecture.*	Pritzker-Preis für Architektur.
1992	Imperial Prize of Architecture, *Japanese Art Association.*	*Prix Impérial d'Architecture de la* Japanese Art Association.	Kaiserlicher Preis für Architektur der *Japanese Art Association.*
1994	Lillian Gish Award.	*1994 Prix Lillian Gish.*	Lillian-Gish-Preis

Museo Guggenheim de Bilbao

1997. Bilbao, España.

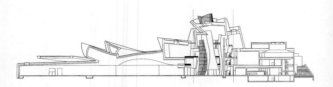

Both the Basque authorities and the representatives of the Guggenheim Foundation were searching for a singular and iconoclastic building that would be a claim to fame in the cultural world and would serve to project the city internationally. What has a greater repercussion in the final shape of the building is Gehry's own special way of working, starting off with models and free maquettes, which are literally transfered to the computer screen to be mathematically analized. The museum is made up of a great central atrium, with a height of 50 meters, crowned with a metalic flower, and three wings orientated to the east, south and west. On the north side, the museum borders on the river and the virtual fourth wing is sectioned so that an enormous glass door can be in its place.

Tant les autorités basques que les représentants de la Fondation Guggenheim plaidaient pour un bâtiment singulier et iconoclaste qui fasse l'éloge du monde culturel, et incarne le rayonnement international de la ville. L'aspect final du bâtiment est avant tout marqué par les méthodes de travail de Gehry, qui part d'esquisses et maquettes libres, fidèlement retranscrites sur ordinateur pour être analysées mathématiquement. Le cœur du musée est un vaste vestibule de 50m de haut, couronné d'une fleur métallique et de trois ailes orientées est, sud et ouest. Côté nord, le musée est attenant à la rivière, et la quatrième aile virtuelle est sectionnée pour faire place à une immense porte vitrée.

Die baskischen Behörden suchten ebenso wie die Repräsentanten der Guggenheim-Stiftung ein einzelnes und ikonoklassisches Gebäude, das sich in eine Reklame für die Welt der Kultur verwandelt und sich für die internationale Wirkung der Stadt eignet. Was eine große Auswirkung auf die endgültige Form des Gebäudes hat, ist die Arbeitsweise von Gehry, die Skizzen und freien Modelle, die sich fast buchstäblich bis zum Computerbildschirm übertragen, um mathematisch analysiert zu werden. Das Museum bildet sich aus einem großen zentralen Atrium, mit einer Höhe von 50 Metern, gekrönt von einer Blume aus Metall und drei Flügeln, die nach Osten, Süden und Westen ausgerichtet sind. Auf der Nordseite des schönen Museums mit dem Fluß und dem virtuellen vierten Flügel befindet sich eine große unterteilte verschiebbare Glastür.

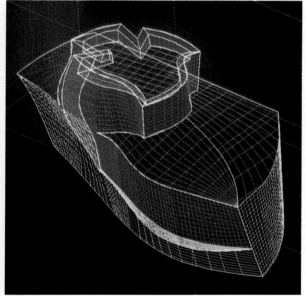

"In this building I begin with very basic organization, for example, a star. It has three points from the center and there would be another if the river was not here"
(Frank O. Gehry).

"Je pars d'une organisation de l'édifice très basique, par exemple, une étoile. Trois branches partent du centre, et il y en aurait une quatrième si ce n'était par la présence de la rivière."
(Frank O. Gehry).

"Ich beginne mit einer sehr grundlegenden Organisation in diesem Gebäude, zum Beispiel, das es ein Stern ist. Es hat drei Spitzen vom Zentrum aus und es hätte noch eine wenn der Fluß nicht da wäre."
(Frank o. Gehry).

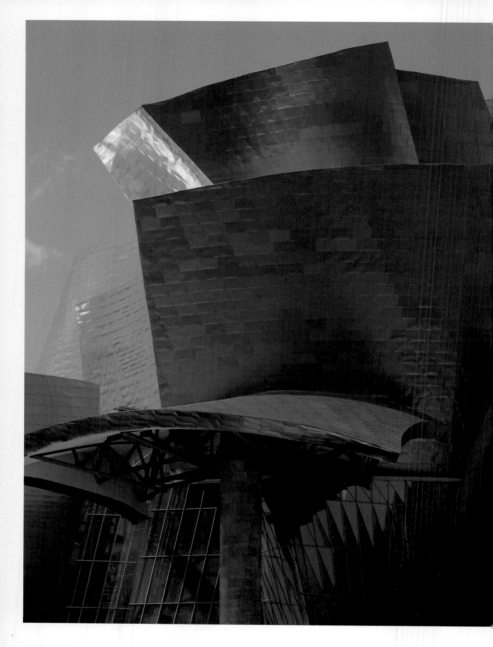

The curved volumes are covered with titanium whereas the rest of the walls are covered with limestone.

Les volumes courbes sont recouverts de titane, et les autres murs de pierre à chaux.

Die abgerundeten Außenseiten sind mit Titanium verkleidet, während der Rest der Mauern mit Kalkstein abgedeckt ist.

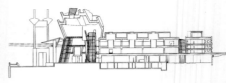

According to the architect himself, some of the scenes from the film "Metropolis" by Fritz Lang inspired the shapes of this museum.

Selon l'architecte lui-même, certaines scènes du film "Métropolis" de Fritz Lang ont inspiré les formes de ce musée.

Dem Architekten zu Folge haben die Szenen aus dem Film "Metropolis" von Fritz Lang zu den Formen dieses Museums inspiriert.

The evolution of these designers, established in Germany, began to be known, when they started thanks to their interventions in things of great scale which entailed the movement of a lot of people such as airports, stations, parking garages and convention centers. Thus, many of their buildings seem like great containers where the role of technology becomes one of the principal design factors. The structural language is usually clear and simple, exploring in some cases the relationship with nature.

La trajectoire de ces architectes basés en Allemagne a débuté par des projets à grande échelle impliquant un important trafic de personnes (aéroports, gares, parkings, champs de foire). Ainsi, la plupart de leurs ouvrages se présentent comme d'immenses conteneurs, où le rôle de la technologie devient l'un des principaux facteurs d'élaboration. Le langage structural est le plus souvent clair et simple, faisant parfois allusion à la nature.

Der Werdegang dieser technischen Zeichner, die sich in Deutschland niedergelassen haben, heißt von Anfang an Interventionen im grossen Maßstab kennenlernen, und zwar dort, wo viel Personenverkehr herrscht, wie Flughäfen, Bahnhöfe, Parkhäuser oder Messegelände. So präsentieren sich viele ihrer Gebäude wie große Container, wo sich das Technologiepapier in eine der Hauptfaktoren des Designs verwandelt. Ihre strukturelle Sprache ist klar und sensibel, und erkundet in einigen Fällen die Beziehung zur Natur.

	Meinhard Von Gerkan was born in Riga, Letonia in 1935. Volkwin Marg was born in Konigsberg, Germany in 1936.	*Meinhard von Gerkan naît à Riga, Lettonie, en 1935. Volkwin Marg naît à Konigsberg, Allemagne, en 1936.*	Meinhard von Gerkan ist 1935 in Riga, Lettland geboren. Volkwin Marg ist 1936 in Königsberg, Deutschland geboren.
1964	Obtained architecture degrees at the *Technische Universität* in Braunschweig, Germany.	*Obtiennent le diplôme d'architecte de la* Technische Universität *de Braunschweig, Allemagne.*	Titel der *Technischen Universität* Braunschweig, Deutschland.
1965	They worked together freelance.	*Travaillent conjointement en autonomes.*	Haben zusammen, aber autonom gearbeitet.
2000	The *International Association of Bridge and Structural Engineering* Award.	*Prix de l'*International Association of Bridge and Structural Engineering.	Preis der *International Association of Bridge and Structural Engeneering.*
2001	Prize DuPont Benedictus of *American Institute of Architects.*	*Prix DuPont Benedictus de l'A-*merican Institute of Architects.	DuPont Benedictus-Preis des *American Institute of Architecture.*
2002	The *Bund Deutscher Architekten* Hamburg 2002 Prize.	*Prix Hambourg 2002 du* Bund Deutscher Architekten.	Hamburg-Preis 2002 des *Bundes Deutscher Architekten.*

New Trade Fair. Leipzig

1996. Leipzig, Deutschland.

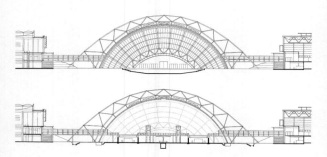

The new drive of the unified Germany to revitalize the old Democratic Republic, made this fair into one of the most important commercial meeting points between eastern and western Europe. The proposal included places for the organization of congresses and meetings parallel to the fair. One of the key points in the development of the complex consisted of separating the circulation into two differentiated levels. A lower level at ground level which serves to receive, orient and distribute the visitors while the higher level provides access to the exhibition and meeting spaces.

Le nouvel élan de l'Allemagne réunifiée pour revitaliser l'ancienne république démocratique fait de cette enceinte l'un des principaux points de rencontre commerciaux entre l'Europe de l'est et l'Europe de l'ouest. Le projet prévoit, parallèlement au centre d'exposition, des salles de congrès et conférence. L'un des points clés de l'ouvrage est le système de séparation des niveaux pour la circulation: un rez-de-chaussée pour l'entrée et l'orientation des visiteurs, et un étage supérieur pour l'accès aux espaces d'exposition et salles de réunion.

Der neue Schwung des vereinten Deutschlands zur Wiederbelebung der ehemaligen DDR verwandelt diese Messe in einen der wichtigsten Geschäftstreffpunkte zwischen Ost- und Westeuropa. Der Vorschlag enthält Orte zur Organisation von Kongressen und Treffen parallel zur Messe. Einer der Schlüsselpunkte in der Entwicklung des Komplexes bestand darin, den Publikumsstrom auf zwei verschiedene Ebenen aufzuteilen. Eine untere Ebene auf der Höhe der Erde, die als Ankunft dient, Orientierung und Verteilung der Besucher, während die andere höherliegende Zugang zur Austellungsfläche und den Konferenzsälen gewährt.

All of the supports of the glass skin are always anchored from the exterior, thus from the interior the glass appears with all of its smoothness, free of obstacles.

Les supports de la verrière sont tous ancrés depuis l'extérieur, la laissant ainsi apparaître dans toute sa pureté depuis l'intérieur, vierge d'obstacles.

Sämtliche Stützen der Glasverkleidung sind immer von außen verankert, so erscheint das Glas von innen immer vollkommen glatt, frei von Hindernissen.

Michael **Graves**

The architect and designer Michael Graves began his career in the middle of the sixties with works circumscribed in the most orthodox way in the Modern Movement but soon he distanced himself from this style when he began to design furniture and all types of objects. His ability for drawing and painting was the foundation on which he developed his architectural talent. Grave's work never leaves you indifferent even though at times it is quite fanciful. It has Mediterranean and classical influences.

L'architecte et designer Michael Graves débuta sa carrière au milieu des années soixante avec des œuvres limitées au Mouvement Moderne le plus orthodoxe. Il s'écarta cependant rapidement de ce style lorsqu'il commença à créer des meubles et des objets divers. Ses aptitudes pour le dessin et la peinture furent la base de l'évolution de son talent architectonique. Les ouvrages de Graves ne laissent jamais indifférent, et en dépit de leur aspect parfois fantastique, leurs influences sont méditerranéennes et classiques.

Der Architekt und Designer Michael Graves begann seine Karriere Mitte der 6oer Jahre mit Werken, die der ortodoxen Modernen Bewegung zugeschrieben werden. Er entfernte sich aber bald von diesem Stil, als er begann Möbel und alle möglichen Objekte zu entwerfen. Seine Geschicklichkeit beim Zeichnen und Malen war die Basis für die Entwickung seines architektonischen Talents.
Die Arbeiten von Graves blieben nie gleichgültig und trotz das sie manchmal ziemlich fantastisch sind, haben sie mediterrane und klassische Einflüsse.

1934	Born in Indianapolis, U.S.A..	*Naît à Indianapolis, Etats-Unis.*	Geboren in Indianapolis, USA.
1959	Obtains a master in architecture from the University of Harvard after having studied at the University of Cincinnati and the University of Ohio.	*Obtient un master en architecture à l'Université de Harvard, après avoir étudié à l'Université de Cincinnati et à celle d'Ohio.*	Erhält einen Master in Architektur an der Universität Havard, nachdem er an den Universitäten von Cincinnati und Ohio studiert hat.
1960-62	Studies at the *American Academy* in Rome.	*Etudie à l'American Academy de Rome.*	Studium an der *American Academy* in Rom.
1964	Founds the Michael Graves & Associates studio.	*Fonde l'agence Michael Graves & Associates.*	Gründet das Büro *Michael Graves & Associates.*
1999	The *National Medal of Arts,* U.S.A.	National Medal of Arts, *Etats-Unis.*	*National Medal of Arts,* USA.
2001	The Gold Medal Award from the *American Institute of Architects.*	*Médaille d'Or de l'American Institute of Architects.*	Goldmedallie des *American Institute of Architects.*

Denver Central Library

1996. Denver, Colorado, U.S.A.

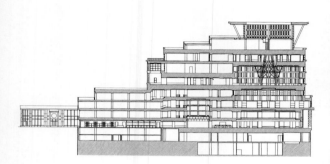

Over the original building, designed by Burnham Hoyt in 1956, Graves realized the enlargement and renovation of the Central Library of the city where scale, coloring and volumetric variety synthesize with the surroundings. Graves attempts to have the project provide an important and symbolic impulse thus recuperating a missing quality in the modern movement: monumentality.

Graves a agrandi et rénové la Bibliothèque Centrale de la ville sur le bâtiment d'origine conçu par Burnham Hoyt en 1956. Echelle, couleur et variété volumétrique s'accordent avec l'environnement. Graves veut charger l'œuvre de symbolisme et de sens, recouvrant ainsi une qualité absente dans le mouvement moderne: la monumentalité.

Über das Originalgebäude, das 1956 von Burnham Hoyt entworfen wurde, hat Graves eine Vergrößerung und Renovierung der Zentralen Stadtbibliothek umgesetzt, wo Maßstab, Farbgebung, und volumetrische Vielfalt mit der Umgebung übereinstimmen.Graves strebt an, daß das Projekt zur symbolischen und bedeutenden Belastung des Gebäudes beiträgt, um eine verlorene Qualität der modernen Bewegung zurückzubekommen: die Monumentalität.

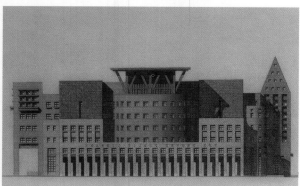

Together with the pure forms that make up the exterior image of the building, the copper protrusion on the roof of the circular tower constitutes a singular element that serves as a counterpoint.

Aux formes pures qui composent l'image extérieure du bâtiment s'oppose la singulière saillie de cuivre de la toiture de la tour circulaire.

Zusammen mit den puren Formen die das äußere Bild des Gebäudes bilden, bildet die Kupfer platte des Daches des runden Turms ein einzelnes Element, das als Gegensatz dient.

University of Cincinnati Engineering Center

1995. Cincinnati, Ohio, U.S.A.

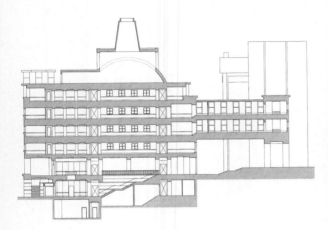

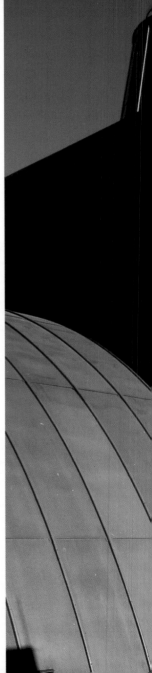

Volumetrically, the building can be understood as the union between a great longitudinal pavilion and four other transversal bodies among which the entrance stands out the most. In spite of the variety of materials (ocher and terra cotta brick) or the shapes of the windows (round or square), the facades evoke a unitarian order.

D'un point de vue volumétrique, l'œuvre peut apparaître comme l'union d'un vaste pavillon longitudinal et de quatre autres corps transversaux, parmi lesquels se détache celui de l'entrée. En dépit de la variété des matériaux (brique rouge et terre cuite) ou des formes des fenêtres (rondes ou carrées), les façades témoignent d'un ordre unitaire.

Volumetrisch kann man das Gebäude als Union zwischen einem großen länglichen Pavillion und anderen transversalen Körpern verstehen, zwischen denen sich der Eingang hervorhebt. Trotz der Materialvielfalt (ockerfarbene Ziegel und Terracota) oder der Fensterformen (rund oder quadratisch), vermitteln die Fassaden eine einheiltiche Ordnung.

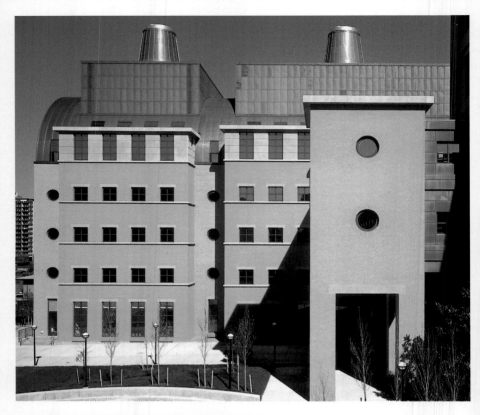

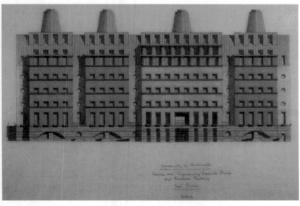

The building, consisting of six floors, is situated perpendicularly to the axis that, from the east, leads to the sqare of the University.

Ce bâtiment de six étages se place perpendiculairement à l'axe menant à la place de l'Université depuis l'est.

Das sechsstöckige Gebäude hängt sich senkrecht an die Achse, die von Osten auf den Platz der Universität zugeht.

On the roof, covered with copper, over a great longitudinal vault, appear suggestive industrial shapes.

Des formes industrielles suggestives apparaissent sur la toiture de cuivre de la vaste voûte longitudinale.

Im kupferbedeckten Dach, über einem großen länglichen Gewölbe erscheinen anregende industrielle Formen.

Heikkinen & **Komonen**

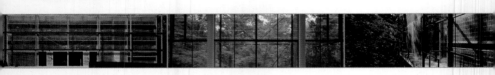

The proposals of these architects generate an interesting project dynamic, which is the result in many cases of careful attention to the surroundings. Thus the projects at first alienate only to later recompose into a clear, formal and functional order. One of the recurring themes in their work is the introduction of natural light which leads us to have unveiled what is occurring inside. Their preference for pure shapes allows them to project attractive, delicately-detailed "box containers".

Les propositions de ces architectes génèrent une dynamique de projet intéressante, et sont le plus souvent fruit d'une attention particulière à l'espace environnant. Les projets se décomposent et se recomposent avec un ordre formel et fonctionnel clair. L'un des thèmes récurrents de leurs œuvres est l'introduction de la lumière naturelle, les menant parfois à dévoiler ce qu'ils ressentent au plus profond. Leur goût pour l'utilisation de formes épurées leur permet d'élaborer de charmantes "caisses" délicatement détaillées.

Die Vorschläge dieser Architekten generieren eine interessante beabsichtigte Dynamik, die in vielen Fällen das Produkt einer sorgfältigen Aufmerksamkeit für die Umgebung ist. So zersetzen sich diese Projekte, um sich dann mit einer klaren, formellen, und funktionalen Ordnung wiederherzustellen. Einsder rückfälligen Themen in seinem Werk ist die Einführung des natürlichen Lichts, welches manchmal verrät, was zwischen ihnen geschieht. Seine Vorliebe für die Nutzung von puren Formen erlaubt ihm, attraktive fein detaillierte "hemmende Kästen" zu entwerfen.

	Mikko Heikkinen was born in Savonlinna and Markku Komonen in Lappeenranta, Finland, in 1949 and 1945, respectively.	*Mikko Heikkinen naît à Savonlinna, et Markku Komonen à Lappeenranta, Finlande, respectivement en 1949 et 1945.*	Mikko Heikkinen ist 1949 in Savonlinna und Markku Komonen 1945 in Lappeenranta, Finnland, geboren. Beide haben ihren Abschluß als Architekt an der *Helsinki University of Technology*, 1975 und 1974, gemacht.
	Degrees in architecture from the *Helsinki University of Technology* in 1975 and 1974 respectively.	*Diplôme d'architecte de l'Helsinki University of Technology, respectivement en 1975 y 1974.*	
1974	They founded *Heikkinen-Komonen-Tiirikainen Architects*.	*Fondent Heikkinen-Komonen-Tiirikainen Architects.*	Gründen *Heikkinen-Komonen-Tiirikainen Architects*.
1978	They founded *heikkinen-Komonen Architects*.	*Fondent Heikkinen-Komonen Architects.*	Gründen *Heikkinen-Komonen Architects*.
1993	European Steel Structure Award.	*Prix de la Structure Européenne d'Acier.*	Prämie der europäischen Stahlstruktur.
1994	*Building of Excellence* from the *Iron Workers Employers Association* in Washington, D.C., Award	*Prix* Building of Excellence *de l'Iron Workers Employers Association de Washington D.C.*	*Building of Excellence*-Prämie der *Iron Workers Employers Association* in Washington, D. C.
2001	Aga Khan Prize.	*Prix Aga Khan.*	Aga Kahn-Preis

Finnish Embassy in Washington D.C.

1994. Washington D.C., U.S.A.

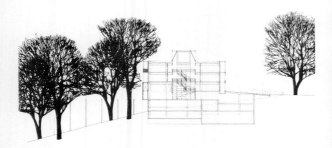

This is a building of paths suspended in the air, difuse limits, osmotic flowing back and forth between exuberant nature in the exterior and the intense chromatics of the interior, of dematerialized parameters transformed into filters of light, in reflective surfaces and in vegetal networks: an architecture which operates by means of some of the most difficult intangibles to convey.

C'est un ouvrage aux parcours suspendus, aux limites diffuses, aux fluences osmotiques entre la nature exubérante de l'extérieur et l'intensité chromatique des intérieurs, aux parements dématérialisés et transformés en filtres de lumière, en surfaces réfléchissantes et en lacis végétaux: une architecture opérant selon une intangibilité difficile à transmettre.

Dies ist ein Gebäude in der Luft hängender Strecken mit verschwommenen Grenzen, mit osmotischen Flüssen zwischen üppiger Natur außen und chromatischer Intensität innen, mit dematerialisierten Parametern, umgewandelt in Lichtfilter, mit reflektierenden Oberflächen und in Pflanzennetzen: Eine Architektur, die mit einigen der am schwierigsten zu übertragenden Immaterialien arbeitet.

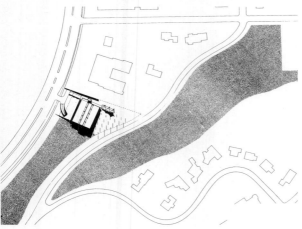

The building combines the rational distribution of the offices with a central space in which catwalks crisscross interrupted over the void, sections of circular stairs and suspended volumes.

Le bâtiment combine une distribution rationnelle des surfaces de bureaux à un espace central, où se croisent des passerelles interrompues au-dessus du vide, des volées d'escaliers circulaires, et des volumes suspendus.

Das Gebäude kombiniert die rationale Verteilung der Bürooberflächen mit einem zentralen Raum, in dem sich über dem Leeren unterbrochene Durchgänge befinden, runde Treppenabschnitte und abgesetzte Außenansichten.

The exterior of the building seems to renounce the introduction of daring shapes in a context in which, by itself, is exuberant, and it is designed with special care being given to detail, evoking the effect of light among the foliage.

L'extérieur du bâtiment paraît renoncer à introduire des formes hasardeuses dans un contexte exubérant en soi, et témoigne d'un soin particulier apporté au détail, évoquant l'effet de la lumière dans les feuillages.

Das Äußere des Gebäudes scheint darauf zu verzichten, bewegte Formen in einem üppigen Kontext einzuführen und zeigt eine spezielle Vorsicht im Detail, den Lichteffekt zwischen dem Laub heraufbeschwörend.

Foibe Housing and Amenity Center for Senior Citizens

1993. Vantaa, Finland.

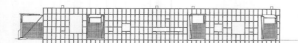

This residence is an example of the singular capacity of the Finnish architects to combine constructive rigor, the search for order, structural purity and pragmatism in design, with the integration into the landscape, the development of the lyric component of the scarce light of the north and respect for nature.

Cette résidence témoigne de la capacité singulière des architectes finlandais à combiner la rigueur constructive, la quête de l'ordre, la pureté structurale et le pragmatisme dans le design, à l'intégration au paysage, au développement de la composante lyrique de la faible lumière du Nord, et au respect de la nature.

Diese Residenz ist ein Beispiel für die einzelnen Fähigkeiten der finnischen Architekten, die bauliche Genauigkeit, die Suche der Ordnung, die strukturelle Reinheit und den Pragmatismus des Designs mit der Integration in die Landschaft, der Entwicklung der lyrischen Komponente des geringen Nordlichts und dem Respekt vor der Natur zu kombinieren.

What stands out is the great volumetric complexity which is attained by means of the disintegration of the buildings into their fundamental elements and their integration into the topography.

La désagrégation des bâtiments dans leurs éléments fondamentaux, et leur intégration dans la topographie, entraînent une grande complexité volumétrique.

Es hebt eine große volumetrische Komplexität hervor, die durch die Zerstreuung der Gebäude in ihren fundamentalen Elementen und ihrer Integration in die Topographie erreicht wird.

Herman **Hertzberger**

Herman Hertzberger is one of the most influential theoriticians of "Structuralism". For this architect and designer, architecture must provide a spacial framework through which users exert influence over the design of the constructions. His works, which include from houses to offices, mold these theories with the creation of social spaces that facilitate the interaction between people and seek transparency in the organization of rooms.

Herman Hertzberger est l'un des théoriciens les plus influents du "Structuralisme". Pour cet architecte et designer, l'architecture doit apporter un cadre spatial où la conception des constructions est marquée par l'influence des usagers. Ces théories se concrétisent dans ses œuvres (maisons, bureaux, écoles), par la création d'espaces sociaux facilitant les échanges interpersonnels, et cherchant la transparence dans l'organisation des pièces.

Herman Hertzberger ist einer der einflussreichsten Theoretiker des "Strukturalismus". Für den Architekten und Designer muß die Architektur einen Platz schaffen, über den die Benutzer Einfluß auf die Entwürfe der Konstruktionen ausüben. Seine Werke, unter ihnen Häuser, Bürogebäude und Schulen, spiegeln diese Theorien mit der Schaffung von Sozialräumen wider, die die Interaktion zwischen den Personen erleichtern und die Transparenz in der Organisation der Wohnräume suchen.

1932	Born in Amsterdam, Netherlands.	*Naît à Amsterdam, Pays-Bas.*	Geboren in Amsterdam, Niederlanden.
1958	Graduates from the *Technical University* of Delft.	*Diplômé de la* Technical University *de Delft.*	Abschluß an der *Technical University* von Delft.
1958	Founds his own studio.	*Fonde son cabinet.*	Gründet sein eigenes Büro.
1974	Fritz-Schumacher Award.	*Prix Fritz-Schumacher.*	Fritz-Schumacher-Preis
1975	Honorary Member of the *Académie Royale de Belgique.*	*Membre honoraire de l'Académie Royale de Belgique.*	Ehrenmitglied der *Académie Royale de Belgique.*
1983	Honorary Member of the *Bund Deutscher Architekten.*	*Membre honoraire du* Bund Deutscher Architekten.	Ehrenmitglied des *Bundes Deutscher Architekten.*
1991	Honorary Member of the *Royal Institute of British Architects.*	*Membre honoraire du* Royal Institute of British Architects.	Ehrenmitglied des *Royal Institute of British Architects.*
	Europa Architettura of the *Fondazione Tetraktis* Award.	*Prix* Europa Architettura *de la* Fondazione Tetraktis.	Europa-Preis für Architektur der *Fondazione Tetraktis.*
1998	Vitruvio 98 Trayectoria Internacional Prize.	*Prix Vitruvio 98 Trajectoire Internationale.*	Vitruvio-Preis 98 für den Internationalen Werdegang.

CENTRAAL BEHEER

1995. Apeldoorn, The Netherlands.

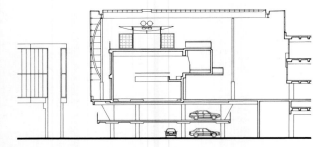

The office building Centraal Beheer was built in 1972 by Herman Hertzberger. Later, minor renovations and enlargements were done until in 1990 it was decided to carry out a major intervention that would combine the construction of new facilities and the integration of all the work carried out beforehand. The intervention of Hertzberger establishes a nexus of union between the original building (CB1) and some adjacent installations acquired by the company (CB2) designed by the architects Kaman and Daavidse.

L'ensemble de bureaux Centraal Beheer *fut construit en 1972 par Herman Hertzberger. Il subit par la suite de petites réorganisations et agrandissements, jusqu'à la décision, en 1990, de réaliser une intervention plus importante, qui combine à la fois la construction de nouvelles dépendances et l'intégration des modifications antérieures.*
Le projet d'Hertzberger établit un trait d'union entre le bâtiment d'origine (CB1), et des installations voisines acquises par l'entreprise (CB2), et dessinées par les architectes Kaman et Davidse.

Das Bürogebäude *Centraal Beheer* wurde 1972 von Herman Hertzberger gebaut. Später folgten kleine Umgestaltungen und Vergrößerungen, bis man 1990 entschied, einen Eingriff von größerer Tragweite durchzuführen, der den Bau neuer Abteilungen und die Integration aller vorher durchgeführten Arbeiten kombiniert. Der Eingriff von Hertzberger stellt eine Verbindung zwischen dem Originalgebäude (CB1) und einigen angrenzenden Einrichtungen her, die die Firma erworben hat (CB2) und die von den Architekten Kaman und Davidse entworfen wurden.

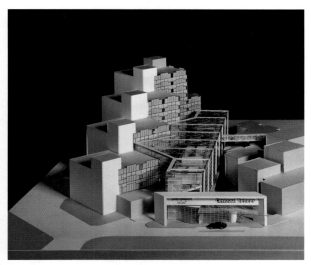

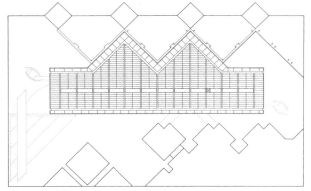

The intervention of Hertzberger introduces, to begin with, a monumental, concrete portico, in line with the street, where the title of the company is displayed.

L'intervention d'Hertzberger introduit, en guise d'entrée, un immense portique en béton parallèle à la rue et portant l'enseigne de l'entreprise.

Der Eingriff Hertzbergers fügt als Eingang einen riesige Säulenhalle aus Beton ein, die neben der Straße aufgestellt ist, an der das Firmenschild steht.

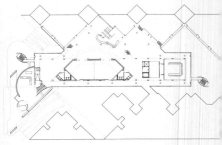

Metal stairs, terraces overlooking the atrium, catwalks that cross the void, vestibules and halls form a heterogeneous succession of spaces immersed in a common order.

Les escaliers en fer, les balcons donnant sur le parvis, les passerelles qui surplombent le vide, les vestibules et salles, forment une succession hétérogène d'espaces, fondue dans un ordre commun.

Metalltreppen, Terassen, die über das Atrium blicken, Durchgänge, die die Leere kreuzen, Vorhallen und Säle die eine heterogene Folge von Räumen mitten in einer gemeinsamen Ordnung schaffen.

CHASSÉ THEATER

1992-1995. Breda, The Netherlands.

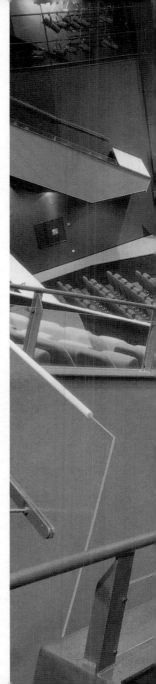

The spacial and program ordering of the theater responds to a fundamentally pragmatic planning, which determines not only the interior activity of the building, but also the exterior image. In the interior, the roundness of the volumes of the auditoriums contrasts with the formal Arabic of the foyer, the true interior street of the complex. The exterior image is characterized by the ondulation of the roof.

L'ordonnance spatiale et programmatique du théâtre répond à une démarche essentiellement pragmatique, déterminant l'activité intérieure du bâtiment, mais également son image extérieure. A l'intérieur, la rotondité des volumes des auditoriums contraste avec le charabia formel du foyer, véritable avenue intérieure du complexe. L'image extérieure est marquée par l'ondulation de la toiture.

Die räumliche Orientierung und Programatik des Theaters antwortet auf einen fundamentalen pragmatischen Ansatz, der nicht nur die innere Aktivität des Gebäudes bestimmt, sondern auch sein äußeres Bild. Im Inneren bildet die Bestimmtheit der Außenansichten der Auditorien einen Kontrast zum formalen Kauderwelsch des Foyers, der wirklichen inneren Straße des Komplexes. Charakteristisch für das äußere Bild ist die Wellenform des Dachs.

In the foyer, the formal chaos of vestibules in the balconies, unobstructed volumes which rise from the floor, catwalks that cut through the void... acquire an intrinsic order with the reticule of colorful concrete pillars.

Dans le foyer, le chaos formel des vestibules en balcons, les volumes exemptés qui surgissent du sol, les passerelles qui sillonnent le vide... s'inscrivent dans un ordre intrinsèque avec le grisé des piliers en béton colorés.

Im Foyer herrscht formales Chaos durch Vorhallen in Balkonen, befreite Außenansichten, die sich vom Boden erheben, Durchgänge, die die Leere durchpflügen...erlangen eine innerliche Ordnung durch das Netz der bunten Betonsäulen.

Steven **Holl**

Steven Holl became known in Europe by his project for the enlargement of the American Library in Berlin.

His work gained attention because of the uniqueness of his arguments that backed up his works, as well as for the techniques that he used. Holl has developed his research on the search for tighter nexus between architectural shapes and the vital contents that they contain, to such a point as to propose new formalizations and terminologies, like "articulated spaces", "silent holes" or "active structures".

Steven Holl se fit connaître en Europe avec son projet d'agrandissement de la Bibliothèque Américaine de Berlin. Ses ouvrages surprirent par la particularité des arguments qui en étaient à la base, ainsi que par les techniques utilisées. Holl a basé sa recherche sur la quête de liens plus étroits entre les formes architectoniques et leurs contenus vitaux. Il proposa ainsi de nouvelles formalisations et significations, tels que les "espaces articulés", les "ouvertures silencieuses" ou les "structures actives".

Steven Holl wurde in Europa mit seinem Projekt zur Vergrößerung der Amerikanischen Bibliothek in Berlin bekannt.

Seine Arbeit zog die Aufmerksamkeit durch die Besonderheit der Argumente auf sich, die seine Werke unterstützen, sowie durch die Techniken, die er verwendet hat. Holl hat seine Recherche durch die Suche nach schmaleren Verbindungen zwischen den architektonischen Formen und die vitalen Inhalte, die sie haben entwickelt, bis zum Vorschlag neuer Formalisierungen und Bedeutungen, wie "artikulierte Räume", "stille Lükken", oder "aktive Strukturen".

1947	Born in Washington, U.S.A..	*Naît à Washington, Etats-Unis.*	Geboren in Washinghton, USA.
1970	Studies architecture in Rome.	*Etudie l'architecture à Rome.*	Studium der Architektur in Rom.
1971	Completes his studies at the University of Washington.	*Termine ses études à l'Université de Washington.*	Beendet sein Studium an der Universität von Washinghton.
1976	Founds *Steven Holl Architects*.	*Fonde* Steven Holl Architects.	Gründet *Steven Holl Architects*.
1998	Alvar Aalto Medal.	*Médaille Alvar Aalto.*	Alvar Aalto-Medallie.
1998	The Chrysler Award for Design.	*Prix Chrysler de l'Innovation dans le Dessin.*	Chrysler-Preis für innovatives Design.
1999	The National Design Award from the *American Institute of Architects*.	*Prix National de Design de l'A-merican Institute of Architects.*	Nationalpreis für Design des *American Institute of Architects*.
2000	*Progressive Architecture* Prize.	*Prix* Progressive Architecture.	Progressive Architecture-Preis

MAKUHARI HOUSING

1996. Chiba, Japan.

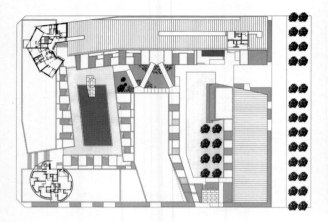

The objective of this project is the ordering of the complete block in the new city of Makuhari which is situated in the Bay of Tokyo. The fabric of this part of the city consists of uniformly closed blocks, with patios in the interior and a medium height of 6-7 floors high. Regarding the volumetric aspect of the plan, Holl takes on the the alteration of this rectangle, bearing in mind sunning criteria, and criteria regarding the opening up of spaces, vision, and the interior patios, thus generating a process of continual alterations of the original block.

L'objectif de ce projet est l'ordonnance de tout un pâté de maisons de la nouvelle ville de Makuhari, dans la baie de Tokyo. Cette partie de la ville est composée de pâté de maisons fermés et réguliers, avec patio intérieur, et d'une hauteur moyenne de 6-7 étages. Dans l'aspect volumétrique de son ordonnance, Holl génère un processus d'altérations continuelles du bloc rectangulaire d'origine, en se basant sur des critères d'ensoleillement, d'ouverture des espaces, de rayons visuels et de patios intérieurs.

Ziel dieses Projekts ist die Ordnung eines kompletten Blocks der Neustadt von Makuhari in der Bucht von Tokio. Das Gewebe dieses Stadtteils besteht aus regulären geschlossenen Blöcken mit Innenhöfen und einer Durchschnittshöhe von sechs bis sieben Stockwerken. Im volumetrischen Aspekt seiner Ordnung schneidet Holl die Veränderung dieses Rechtecks an, basierend auf Kriterien des in die Sonne Bringens, der Öffnung der Plätze, der sichtbaren und der Innenhöfe, der Generierung eines kontinuierlichen Veränderungsprozesses des Originalblocks.

The different water colors show the formal nature of the buildings.

Les différentes aquarelles montrent l'aspect formel des bâtiments.

Die verschiedenen Aquarelle zeigen den formalen Aspekt der Gebäude.

Notwithstanding the continuous alterations of the original block Holl never veers from the initial scheme.

En dépit des constantes altérations du bloc d'origine, Holl respecte le projet initial.

Trotz der kontinuierlichen Veränderungen des Originalblocks hört Holl niemals auf sich von den ursprünglichen Ansätzen zu entfernen.

From the encounter between the heavy base and the light structure springs forth a situation of equilibrium, which corresponds to the oriental idea of "equilibrium between opposites".

De la rencontre entre la base lourde et la structure légère naît une situation d'équilibre correspondant au concept oriental d'"équilibre des opposés".

Durch das Zusammentreffen der schweren Basis und der leichten Struktur entsteht ein Gleichgewicht, das mit dem orientalischen Gedanken vom "Gleichgewicht der Gegensätze" übereinstimmt.

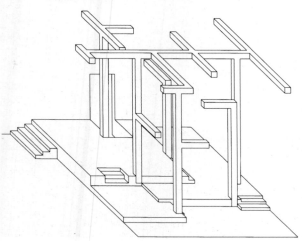

CHAPEL OF ST. IGNATIUS

1997. Seattle, U.S.A.

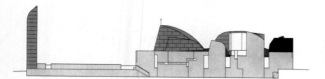

Situated in the campus of the University of Seattle, St. Ignatius chapel is for the Jesuit community in this campus. The constructed body of the chapel is found in the center of a virtual, four-arm cross, all of which are occupied by great, green, rectangular surfaces, in such a way that the church seems to be the result of the intersection of them.

Située sur le campus de l'Université de Seattle, la chapelle St. Ignatius est destinée à sa communauté jésuite. Le corps de la chapelle se trouve au cœur d'une croix virtuelle à quatre branches, chacune étant un immense espace vert rectangulaire. L'église apparaît donc comme le résultat de leur point d'intersection.

Auf dem Campus der Universität von Seattle plaziert, ist die Kapelle St. Ignazius für die Jesuitengemeinde der Universität bestimmt. Der Körper, aus dem die Kapelle gebaut wurde, befindet sich ein einem virtuellen Kreuz aus vier Armen, alle vier mit großen grünen Oberflächen mit rechteckigem Umfang, so daß die Kirche das Ergebnis ihres Schnittpunktes zu sein scheint.

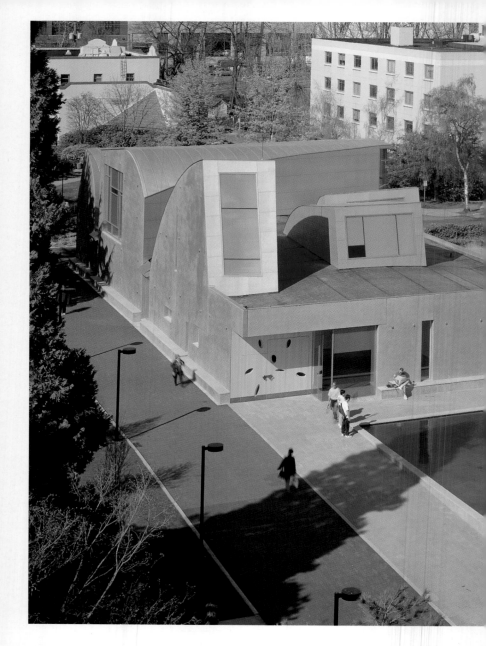

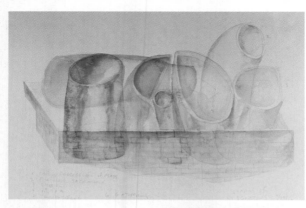

The plan of the chapel takes as its starting point the rectangular perimeter and the nave is situated longitudinally.

Le plan de la chapelle s'appuie sur son périmètre rectangulaire, et la nef principale est placée dans le sens longitudinal.

Das Kapellengeschoß nimmt als Ausgangspunkt seinen rechteckigen Umfang, und das Hauptschiff befindet sich länglich dazu.

In this work the references to Le Corbussier are obvious in respect to the choice of materials and to Aalto in regards to the geometry used.

Les références à Le Corbusier pour le choix des matériaux, et à Aalto pour la géométrie, sont évidentes dans cette œuvre.

In diesem Werk sind die Refenrenzen von Le Corbussierdurch die Wahl der Materialien offensichtlich, und die von Aalto durch die verwendete Geometrie.

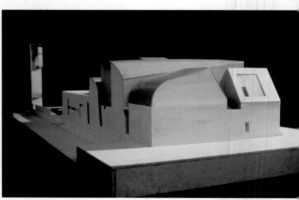

The square pond is conceived as a place of meditation.

Le bassin rectangulaire est conçu comme un espace de méditation.

Der rechteckige Glasraum ist als Meditationsraum vorgesehen.

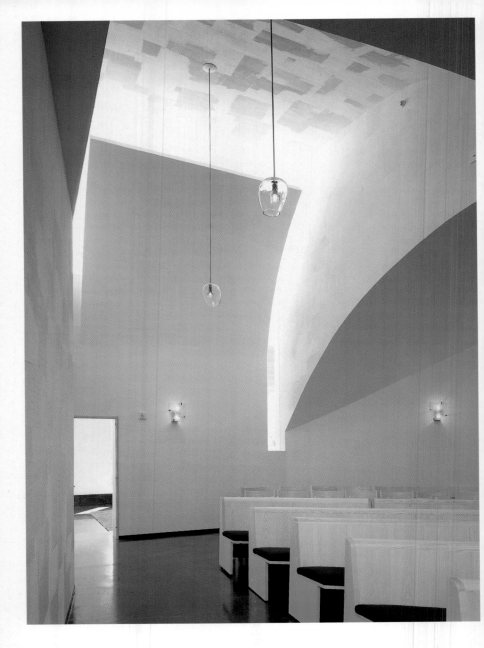

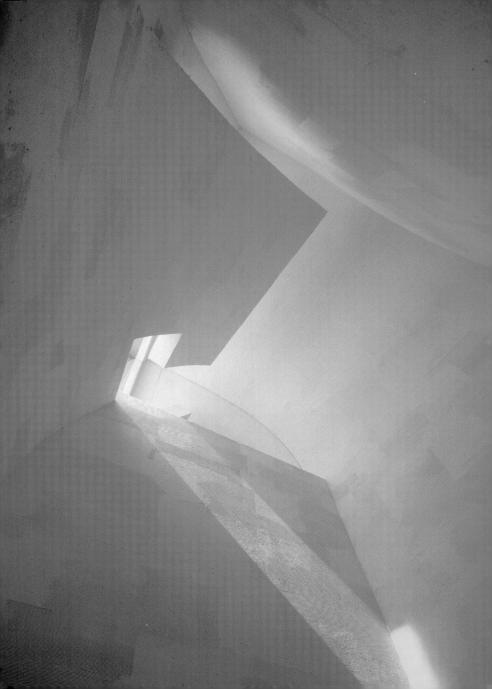

Fukuoka Housing

1991. Fukuoka, Japan.

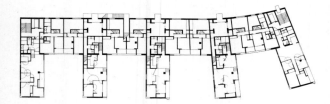

It consists of a complex of 28 dwellings situated in a peripheral area of Fukuoka, which basically constitutes a unitarian block, although dealt with according to the aforementioned concepts of "articulated space" and "empty space". The block is organized around four great patios oriented to the south, whose lower surface is made up of a sheet of water. These four holes are articulated with the rest of the complex by means of their connection with four other porched spaces which open to the interior of the block.

Cet ensemble de 28 habitations, situé dans une zone périphérique de Fukuoka, constitue un bloc essentiellement unitaire, bien que traité selon deux concepts mentionnés précédemment: "espace articulé" et "espace vide". Le bloc s'organise autour de quatre vastes patios orientés sud, dont la surface inférieure est formée d'une nappe d'eau. Ces quatre ouvertures s'articulent au reste de l'ouvrage par une connexion avec d'autres porches menant à l'intérieur du pâté de maison.

Es handelt sich um einen Komplex mit 28 Wohnungen am Stadtrand von Fukuoka, die einen grundsätzlich einzigartigen Block bilden, auch wenn er nach zwei bereits erwähnten Konzepten behandelt wird: "artikulierter Raum" und "leerer Raum". Der Block ordnet sich um vier große Innenhöfe, die alle nach Süden ausgerichtet sind, deren Oberfläche aus einer Wasserfolie besteht. Diese vier Lücken artikulieren mit dem Rest des Komplexes durch ihre Verbindung mit anderen Plätzen durch Arkaden im Inneren des Blockes

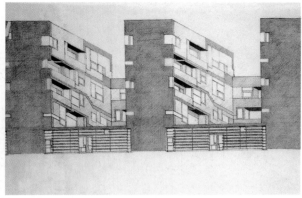

The silent hollows oriented south and the porches, a beehive of activity, oriented north are connected by a a one-floor-high slit.

Les ouvertures silencieuses orientées sud, et les porches abritant l'activité orientés nord, sont reliés par une fente d'une hauteur d'un étage.

Die ruhigen, nach Süden ausgerichteten Lückenund die belebten Verandas, die nach Norden ausgerichtet sind, sind durch einen Spalt mit einem oberen Stockwerk verbunden.

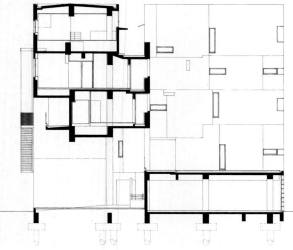

In the interior of the dwellings the mobile, folding screens, the closets and the pivotal soffits are adaptable depending on the season, the time and the moment of the day.

A l'intérieur des habitations, les cloisons mobiles, les armoires et plafonds pivotants s'adaptent selon les saisons, le temps, ou l'heure de la journée.

Im Inneren der Wohnungen passen sich die mobilen Wandschirme, die Schränke und die zentralen Dekkenleuten nach Jahreszeit, Wetter oder Tageszeit an.

Arata **Isozaki**

Arata Isozaki is one of the principal Japanese architects of the generation posterior to Kenzo Tange, and he is considered to be the unchallenged master of the following generations. In the last few years Isozaki has developed research on the dialogue between shapes and western construction procedures and those more common to oriental culture. By doing so he occupies one of the most critical positions but also at the same time, most coherent, in the revision process of the dogmas of modern architecture.

Arata Isozaki est l'un des principaux architectes japonais de la génération postérieure à celle de Kenzo Tange. Il est considéré comme le maître incontesté des générations suivantes. Ces dernières années, Isozaki s'est penché sur une étude du dialogue entre les formes et les processus de construction occidentaux, et ceux plus propres à la culture orientale, occupant ainsi l'une des positions les plus critiques et cohérentes à la fois dans la révision des dogmes de l'architecture moderne.

Arata Isozaki ist einer der japanischen Hauptarchitekten der nachfolgenden Generation von Kenzo Tange, und er wird ohne Zweifel als Meister der folgenden Generationen betrachtet. In den letzten Jahren hat Isozaki eine Untersuchung über den Dialog zwischen den Formen und den westlichen Konstruktionsverfahren und viel näherliegend, den orientalischen durchgeführt und nimmt damit eine der kritischsten und gleichzeitig kohärentesten Positionen im Revisionsprozeß der Dogmen der modernen Architektur ein.

1931	Born in Oubun, Japan.	*Naît à Oubun, Japon.*	Geboren in Oubun, Japan.
1961	Completes his doctorate in architecture at the University of Tokyo.	*Doctorat d'architecture de l'Université de Tokyo.*	Beendet seine Doktorarbeit in Architektur an der Univrsität von Tokio.
1963	Founds *Isozaki Arata & Associates.*	Fonde *Isozaki Arata & Associates.*	Gründet *Isozaki Arata & Associates.*
1970	Special Award from the *Architectural Institute of Japan.*	*Prix Spécial de l'*Architectural Institute of Japan.	Sonderpreis des *Architectural Institute of Japan.*
1986	Gold Medal from the *Royal Institute of British Architects.*	*Médaille d'Or du* Royal Institute of British Architects.	Goldmedallie des *Royal Institute off British Architects.*
1988	Asahi Prize.	*Prix Asahi.*	Asahi-Preis
1988	Arnold W. Brunner Award from the *American Academy and Institute of Arts and Letters.*	*Prix Arnold W. Brunner de l'*American Academy and Institute of Arts and Letters.	Arnold W. Brunner-Preis der *American Academy and Institute of Arts and Letters.*
1996	León de Oro at the *Biennale d'Architettura* in Venice.	*Lion d'Or de la* Biennale d'Architettura *de Venecia.*	Golderner Löwe auf der *Biennnale d'Architettura de Venecia.*

Japanese Art Center in Cracow

1994. Cracow, Poland.

Built on the request of the film-maker Andrej Wajda, this small pavilion was supposed to house an important collection of Japanese art belonging to the National Museum of Poland. Owing to its small dimensions, owing to its location and owing to the nature of the program, it appears as a recreation of the traditional Japanese constructions located in rural surrounding, with their building traditions and their symbolic weight. The construction consists of two floors of which the main one is the upper which leads directly to the access. The lower floor houses the secondary rooms and a large multi-use hall.

Construit à la demande du réalisateur Andrej Wajda, ce petit pavillon devait héberger une importante collection d'art japonais appartenant au Musée National de Pologne. Par ses dimensions, son emplacement et la nature de son programme, il rompait avec les constructions japonaises traditionnelles situées en milieu rural, avec leurs méthodes de construction et leur charge symbolique. Des deux étages du bâtiment, l'étage supérieur est le principal, auquel l'accès est direct. A l'étage inférieur se trouvent des dépendances secondaires, ainsi qu'une grande salle à usages divers.

Dieser kleine Pavillion, der im Auftrag des Kinoregisseurs Andrej Wajda gebaut wurde, sollte eine wichtigeSammlung japanischer Kunst beherbergen, die dem Nationalmuseum von Polen gehört. Wegen seiner kleinen Dimensionen, wegen seiner Lage und wegen der Natur seines Programmes präsentierte er sich wie eine Nachahmung der japanischen Konstruktionen, die in traditionell ländlichen Umgebungen plaziert werden, mit ihren Bautraditionen und ihrer symbolischen Bedeutung. Die Konstruktion hat zwei Stokkwerke, von denen das Hauptstockwerk das höhere ist, zu welchem sie direkt Zugang gewährt. Das untere Stockwerk beherbergt zweitrangige Räume und einen großen Mehrzwecksaal.

The majority of the perimeter of the building has an undulant shape so the resulting arris of the intersection of planes is not rectilinear in any part.

La majorité du périmètre du bâtiment adopte une forme ondulée. L'arête résultant de l'intersection des plans n'est donc jamais rectiligne.

Der Umfang des gebauten Körpers nimmt in seinem Hauptteil eine wellenförmige Form an, mit der die resultierende Kante der Ebenenschnittpunkte in keinem Abschnitt geradlinig ist.

In the pavilion Isozaki shows his interest in complex roof undulations as a way of fitting his constructions into the surroundings.

Pour Isozaki, les ondulations complexes des toitures du pavillon permettent de l'insérer dans le paysage.

Isozaki spiegelt in dem Pavillon sein Interesse für komplexe Wellungen der Dächer als Art und Weise seine Konstruktionen in die Landschaft einzufügen, wider.

Kyoto Concert Hall

1995. Kyoto, Japan.

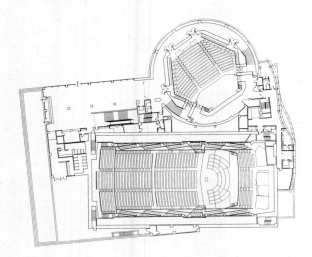

The constuction of the Kyoto concert hall is to commemorate the 1,200 year anniversary of the founding of the city. The focus of the project puts all of its emphasis on two main aspects: on the one hand, the volumetric definition of the complex in relation to the immediate urban complex. On the other hand, the examination of the most compromising aspect of the program: the dimensions, the spatial configuration and the arrangement of the seating in the two large halls required there, one of 1,800 seats and the other of 500.

La construction de la salle de concerts de Kyoto correspond à la commémoration des 1200 ans de la fondation de la ville. Le projet repose avant tout sur deux aspects principaux. D'un côté, la définition volumétrique de l'ensemble par rapport à son environnement urbain immédiat. D'un autre, l'examen de l'aspect le plus engagé du programme: les dimensions, la configuration spatiale, et la disposition des fauteuils des deux grandes salles requises, une de 1800, et une autre de 500 places.

Die Konstruktion des Konzertsaals von Kyoto antwortet auf die 1200 Jahr-Feier der Stadtgründung. Der Ansatz des Projektes setzt seinen ganzen Nachdruck auf die zwei Hauptaspekte: Einerseits die volumetrische Definition des Komplexes in der Beziehung mit dem angrenzenden urbanen Kontext. Andererseits die Prüfung des schwierigsten Aspektes des Programms: Die Dimensionen, die räumliche Aufteilung und die Anordnung des Parketts in den zwei erforderlichen großen Sälen, einer mit 1800 Sitzplätzen und der andere mit 500.

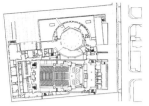

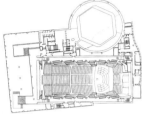

The complex appears as a macle of three bodies, each one with a distinct orientation and globally housed by one unitarian roof.

L'ensemble apparaît comme une macle à trois corps, chacun avec une orientation différente, et tous regroupés sous une seule toiture unitaire.

Der Komplex ist wie eine symetrische Verbindung von zwei Kristallen aus drei Körpern gestaltet, jede von ihnen mit einer anderen Ausrichtung und global mit einem einzigen einheitlichen Dach abgedeckt.

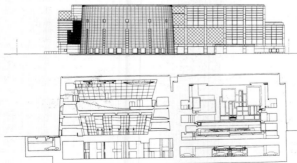

The vestibules and exterior areas
of the halls are orientated in ac-
cordance with the neighboring
buildings.

*Les vestibules et espaces extérieurs
aux salles sont orientés selon la
maille des constructions voisines.*

Die Vorhallen und Zonen außerhalb
der Säle orientieren sich am Netz
der Nachbargebäude.

This building is a reflection of the relationship of interior spaces and the city where they are located.

Cette œuvre se présente comme une réflexion sur le lien entre les espaces intérieurs et la ville qui en est le décor.

Dieses Gebäude präsentiert sich wie eine Reflexion über die Beziehung der Innenräume und der Stadt in der es sich einschreibt.

DOMUS. CASA DEL HOMBRE

1995. A Coruña, España.

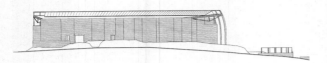

Near the Hercules lighthouse, is the House of Man, the Domus, an interactive museum for understanding better the human body. This project, at the beginnning, had a problem of scale. The building attempts to become landmark which is able to dialogue with the neighboring Hercules lighthouse, thus the attempt to build a simple but forceful shape since it would be viewed from afar. Other considerations to be added were the climatic characteristics of the Galician coast known for its strong winds and strong waves. In response to both premises, climate and scale, a curved wall was created as if it were inflated by the wind, with very few apertures.

Près du Phare de la Tour d'Hercule se trouve la Maison de l'Homme, la Domus, musée interactif sur la réalité du corps humain. Le point de départ du projet était un problème d'échelle. L'édifice prétend devenir un jalon capable de dialoguer avec la Tour d'Hercule voisine, d'où la volonté d'ériger une forme simple, mais assez percutante pour être vue de loin. A ces considérations sur l'implantation, s'ajoutèrent les caractéristiques climatiques de la côte galicienne, connue pour ses rafales de vent et ses fortes vagues. Pour répondre à ces prémisses, on élabora un mur courbe, tel gonflé par le vent, avec très peu d'ouvertures.

Neben dem Leuchtturm von Herkules befindet sich das *Casa del Hombre*, das *Domus*, ein interaktives Museum zum besseren Verständnis des menschlichen Körpers. Dieses Projekt hatte als Ausgangspunkt ein Problem mit dem Maßstab. Das Gebäude versucht sich in einen Meilenstein zu verwandeln, der in der Lage ist, sich mit dem nahen Herkules Leuchtturm zu unterhalten, darum der Wille eine einfache aber schlagkräftige Form zu bauen, die von weitem gesehen wird. Zieht man all das zur Einführung in Betracht, summieren sich die Charakteristika der galizischen Küste, die bekannt ist für ihre starken Winde und Wellen. Entspricht man beiden Vorraussetzungen, Klima und Maßstab, bildet sich eine kurvenreiche Mauer, die wenn sie vom Wind aufgeblasen werden würde wenige Öffnungen hätte.

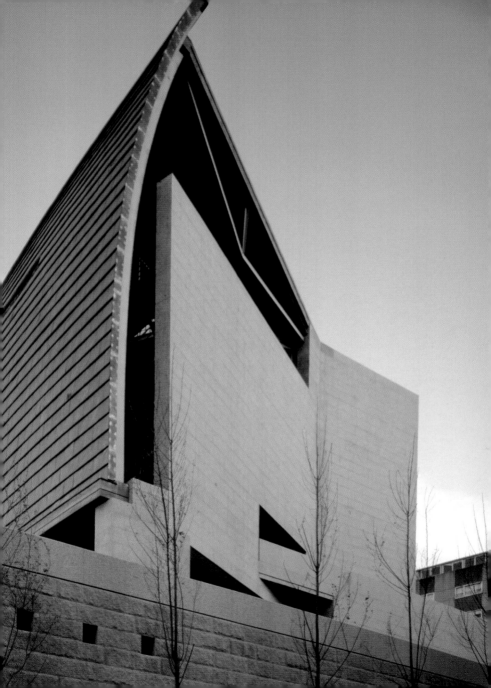

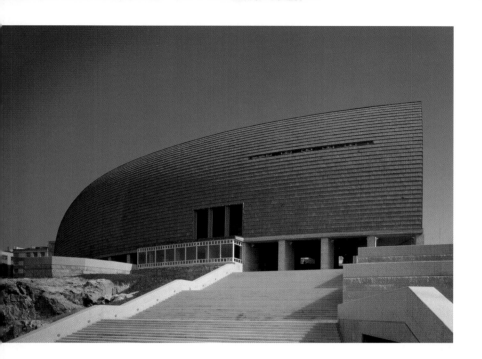

The wall is made up of sections of concrete which after being imper-neabilized are covered with green-sh shale.

Le mur est composé de pièces de béton qui, une fois imperméabilisé, fut recouvert d'ardoises verdâtres.

Die Mauer formiert sich aus Beton-tücken die, einmal imprägniert, mit grünlichen Schieferstücken verkleidet wurde.

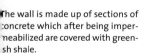

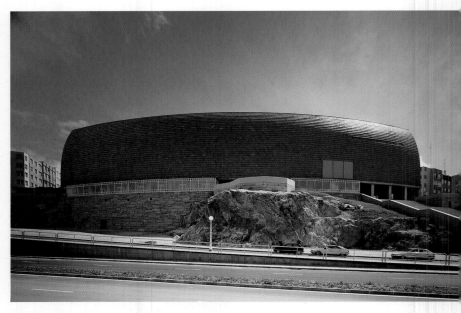

The interior is a continuous exhibi
tion space which adapts to the to
pography thanks to a series o
ramps which successively connec
the three levels of the museum
space.

L'intérieur est une salle d'exposition
continue, qui s'adapte à la topogra
phie grâce à une série de rampe
unissant successivement les trois ni
veaux du musée.

Das Innere ist ein ununterbroche
ner erläuternder Raum, der sicha
die Topographie dank einer Reihe
von aufeinanderfolgenden Ram
pen, die die drei Ebenen des Mu
seums vereinen, anpaßt.

The interior illumination is achieved exclusively by means of a roof skylight. This assures light and permits the introversion of the exhibition room in respect to the sea.

L'illumination intérieure n'est obtenue que par la longue lucarne de la toiture. Elle fournit la lumière, et permet l'introversion de la salle d'exposition par rapport à la mer.

Die Innenbeleuchtung wird lediglich durch die offenen Dachluken erreicht. Das sichert das Licht und erlaubt die Introvertiertheit des Ausstellungssaales hinsichtlich des Meeres.

Toyo **Ito**

The architecture of Atoyo Ito is known for its search for the fusion of the material with the virtual, a proposal which has converted him into a creator of conceptually extreme and revolutionary constructions. Adjectives such as light, luminous, or transparent have been used to describe his style, which tries to respond to the problems of mankind with his present technified surroundings and proposes new solutions for adapting ourselves to the transformations of the great contemporary cities.

L'architecture de Toyo Ito est connue pour sa quête d'une fusion du matériel et du virtuel, un dessein qui fit de lui un créateur de réalisations révolutionnaires, et extrêmes dans leurs concepts. Des qualificatifs tels que léger, lumineux ou transparent, ont souvent décrit son style, qui tente de répondre aux problèmes de l'homme au sein de son environnement industrialisé, et propose des solutions pour qu'il s'adapte aux mutations des grandes villes contemporaines.

Die Architektur von Toyo Ito ist fü die Fusion des Materials mit der Virtuellen bekannt, eine Absicht, di ihn in einen Schöpfer von begriff lich extremen und revolutionäre Bauten verwandelt. Adjektive wi leicht, strahlend oder transparer wurden verwendet, um seinen St zu beschreiben, der versucht, au die Probleme der Menschen mit il rer aktuellen technischen Umge bung zu antworten und neue Lö sungen vorschlägt, um uns an di Veränderungen der großen zeitge nössischen Städte zu gewöhnen.

1941	Born in Nagano, Japan.	Naît à Nagano, Japon.	Geboren in Nagano, Japan
1965	Completes his architecture studies at the University of Tokyo.	Termine ses études d'architecture à l'Université de Tokyo.	Beendet sein Architekturstudium an der Universität von Tokio.
1965-69	He works in the *Kiyonori kikutaki & Associates* studio.	Travaille pour l'agence Kiyonori Kikutake & Associates.	Arbeitet im Büro von *Kiyonor Kikutake & Associates*.
1971	Founds his own studio the *Urban Robot (URBOT)* in Tokyo.	Fonde son propre cabinet, l'Urban Robot (URBOT), *Tokyo*.	Gründetsein eigenes Büro, da *Urban Robot (URBOT)* in Tokic
1979	Changes the name of his studio to *Toyo Ito And Associates*.	Change le nom de son agence pour Toyo Ito and Associates.	Ändert den Namen seines Bü ros in *Toyo Ito and Associates*
1986	*Architecture Institute of Japan Award.*	*Prix de l'*Architecture Institute of Japan.	Preis des *Architecture Institut of Japan.*
2000	Arnold W. Brunner Award from the *American Academy and Institute of Arts and Letters.*	*Prix Arnold W. Brunner de l'*American Academy and Institute of Arts and Letters.	Arnold W. Brunner-Preis *de American Academy* und de *Institite of Arts and Letters.*
	Honorary Member of the *American Institute of Architects.*	*Membre honoraire de l'*American Institute of Architects.	Ehrenmitglied des *America Institute of Architects.*

1997. Nagaoka, Japan.

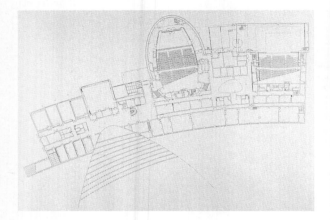

In the outskirts of the Japanese city of Nagaoka on the banks of the river Shinano in a place with a view of the mountains of Echigo, this building completes an extensive offer of an extensive cultural and educational area. Within a large plot, the building positions itself from the creation of its own topography. Apart from organizing the surface parking towards the west, the building takes possession of the terrain by means of topographical changes.

Le bâtiment se trouve sur la périphérie de la ville japonaise de Nagaoka, sur les rives du fleuve Shinano, d'où se découpent au loin les montagnes d'Echigo. Il complète une large zone culturelle et éducative. L'œuvre est érigée sur un vaste terrain, et s'élève à partir de la création d'une topographie propre. Mise à part l'espace réservé au stationnement en surface vers l'ouest, l'ouvrage prend possession du terrain grâce à des changements topographiques.

In der Pheripherie der japanischen Stadt Nagaoka, am Ufer des Flußes Shinano, an einem Ort mit entferntem Blick auf die Berge von Echigo, vervollständigt das Gebäude das große Angebot einer weitläufigen Kultur- und Lernzone. Auf einem großen Grundstück, nimmt das Gebäude eine Stellung mit der Schaffung einer eigenen Topographie ein. Abgesehen von der Organisation des Platzes, der für den Parkplatz an der Oberfläche im Osten benötigt wird, nimmt das Gebäude auf dem Grundstück seine Position über topographische Veränderungen ein.

The simple plan of corridors which offers access to the different pieces, is enriched by the distinct expansions which it experiences in contact with them.

La simplicité du schéma de couloir donnant accès aux différentes pièces est enrichie par les élargissements qu'il subit à leur contact.

Das einfache Schema des Korridors gibt Zugang zu den veschiedenen Stücken, es bereichert sich über die verschiedenen Verbreiterungen, die es im Kontakt mit ihnen erleidet.

Kengo **Kuma**

Kengo Kuma is, together with Shigeru Ban y Kazuyo Sejima, one of the most interesting Japanese architects from the generation posterior to Tadao Ando and Toyo Ito. His latest works show an unusual capacity for working with the least apprehensible elements of architecture: light, water, air and landscape. His projects are light and search for transparency. Kengo Kum asserts that architecture must establish a new relationship between subject and object, which overcomes the idea of building as a representative object.

Kengo Kuma est, avec Shigeru Ban et Kazuyo Sejima, l'un des architectes japonais les plus intéressants de la génération postérieure à Tadao Ando et Toyo Ito. Ses dernières œuvres témoignent d'une aptitude exceptionnelle à travailler avec les éléments les moins maîtrisables de l'architecture: la lumière, l'eau, l'air et le paysage. Ses projets sont légers, et recherchent la transparence. Selon Kengo Kuma, l'architecture doit créer une nouvelle relation entre sujet et objet, et dépasser le concept d'édifice comme objet représentatif.

Kengo Kuma ist, zusammen mit Shigeru Ban und Kazuyo Sejima, einer der interessantesten japanischen Architekten der Generation nach Tadao Ando und Toyo Ito. Seine letzten Werke zeigen eine ungewöhnliche Kapazität zur Arbeit mit den am wenigsten begreifenbaren Elementen der Architektur: Licht, Wasser, Luft und Landschaft. Seine Projekte sind leicht und suchen Transparenz. Kengo Kuma meint, daß die Architektur eine neue Beziehung zwischen Subjekt und Objekt herstellen muß, die den Gedanken des Gebäudes als repräsentatives Objekt überwindet.

1954	Born in Kanagawa, Japan.	Naît à Kanagawa, Japon.	Geboren in Kanagawa, Japan.
1979	Master in architecture from the University of Tokyo.	Master d'architecture de l'Université de Tokyo.	Master in Architektur an der Universität von Tokio.
1987	Founds the *Spatial Design Studio* office.	Fonde le cabinet Spatial Design Studio.	Gründet das Büro *Spatial Design Studio*.
1990	Founds *Kengo Kuma & Associates*.	Fonde Kengo Kuma & Associates.	Gründet *Kengo Kuma & Associates*.
1995	Grand Prize of design from the *Japanese Society of Commercial Space Designers* (JCD).	Grand prix de Design de la Japanese Society of Commercial Space Designers (JCD).	Großer Design-Preis der *Japanese Society of Commercial Space Designerss (JCD)*.
1997	Award from the *Architectural Institute of Japan*.	Prix de l'Architectural Institute of Japan.	Preis des *Architectural Institute of Japan*.
1997	Dupont Benedictus Award, *American Institute of Architects*.	Prix DuPont Benedictus, American Institute of Architects.	DuPont Benedictus-Preis, *American Institute of Architects*.
2000	Design Award from the *Tohoku Chapter* of the *Architectural Institute of Japan*.	Prix de design du Tohoku Chapter de l'Architectural Institute of Japan.	Design-Preis des *Tohoku Chapter* des *Architectural Institute of Japan*.

Yusuhara Visitor's Center

1994. Takaoka, Japan.

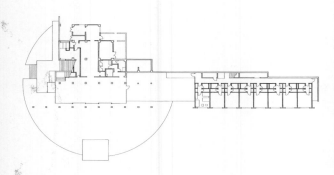

The essential philosophy of this project – a restaurant and lodge for visitors – is a commitment of architecture with nature, establishing a dialectic with nature. The platform of the restaurant has a direct relationship with the lamina of water of the pond, as if it were a pier. The roof is a ribbed structure with a lune profile, covered with cedar in the lower and lateral part, and covered with stainless steel in the top part.

La vocation première de ce projet - un restaurant et une auberge pour les visiteurs - est le compromis de l'architecture avec le paysage, déployant une réelle dialectique avec la nature. La plate-forme du restaurant se conjugue à la nappe d'eau de l'étang, tel un embarcadère.

Die wesentliche Berufung dieses Projekts –ein Restaurant und Herberge für Besucher– ist der Kompromiss der Architektur mit der Landschaft, der einen Dialekt mit der Natur entfaltet. Die Plattform des Restaurantes hat eine direkte Verbindung zur Wasserfolie des Teiches, als würde es sich um eine Landungsbrücke handeln.

The roof is a ribbed structure with a lune shape, covered with cedar wood on the lower and lateral part, and plated with stainless steel on the upper part.

La toiture est une structure de cintres en forme de fuseaux. Sa partie inférieure et latérale est recouverte de bois de cèdre, et sa partie supérieure, d'une plaque d'acier inoxydable.

Das Dach ist eine Struktur aus lamellen mit einem Spindelprofil, verkleidet mit Zedernholz im unteren und seitlichen Teil, und mit rostfreien Stahlplatten im oberen Teil.

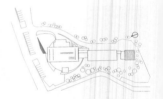

In the space between the elliptical roof and the pond all the elements seem to float.

Dans l'espace entre la toiture elliptique et l'étang, tous les éléments semblent flotter.

In dem Raum zwischen dem eliptischen Dach und dem Teich scheinen alle Elemente zu schweben.

1995. Shizuoka, Japan.

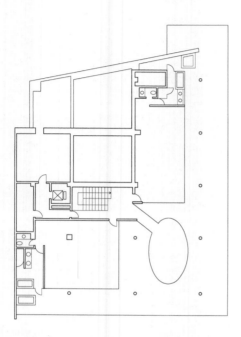

The Water and Glass House, whose principal use is to receive guests, has a total constructed surface of 1,125 square meters in three floors and occupies half of a ground of 1,281 square meters. It is situated on the edge of a cliff over the coast of Atami, overlooking the Pacific Ocean.

La Maison d'Eau et de Verre, dont l'usage principal est la réception d'invités, a une superficie totale de 1.125 m² , répartie sur trois étages, et occupe la moitié de la surface d'un terrain de 1.281 m². Elle se trouve au bord d'une falaise, sur la côte d'Atami, face à l'Océan Pacifique.

Das Haus aus Wasser und Glas, dessen Hauptnutzung die Aufnahme von geladenen Gästen ist, hat eine 1125 m² große Fläche, auf drei Etagen verteilt, und es belegt die Hälfte eines Grundstücks mit 1281 m². Es befindet sich am Rand einer Steilküste über der Küste von Atami, am Pazifischen Ozean.

A system of transparent and translucent skins create a very complex visual relationship in which shadows, reflections and duplicities that allow the paths to be outlined and dilute the division between interior and exterior.

Un système de couches transparentes et translucides crée une relation visuelle très complexe dans laquelle ombres, reflets et duplicités permettent de définir les parcours, diluant la séparation entre intérieur et extérieur.

Ein System aus transparenten und lichtdurchlässigen Verkleidungen schafft eine sehr komplexe visuelle Beziehung, in der Schatten, Reflexe und Duplizität die Definition einer Strecke erlauben, die die Teilung zwischen innen und außen auflöst.

Kisho **Kurokawa**

The basic idea of Kurokawa is to pose proposals, from industrial design to urbanism, in which technological advances and and the system for aggregating residencial capsules, is basic. "Standardization was important in industrial societies, but in the present society of the information, identity and differentiation acquire a more relevant role", Kurokawa points out.

L'idée de base de Kurokawa est l'élaboration de propositions (du design industriel à l'urbanisme), qui reposent sur les avancées technologiques et les systèmes d'agrégation de capsules résidentielles. Kurokawa explique: "La standardisation a dominé dans une société industrielle. Mais, dans la société actuelle de l'information, l'identité et la différence jouent un rôle plus important".

Die Grundidee von Kurokawa ist es Vorschläge vom Industriedesign bis zur Stadtplanung anzugehen, bei denen der technologische Fortschritt und das Hinzufügen von Wohnkapseln grundlegend sind. "Standarisieren war wichtig in einer Industriegesellschaft, aber, in der aktuellen Informationsgesellschaft, verlangen die Identität und die Differenz eine relevanteres Papier," erklärt Kurokawa.

1934	Born in Nagoya, Japan.	Naît à Nagoya, Japon.	Geboren in Nagoza, Japan.
1957	Graduates from the University of Kioto.	Diplômé de l'Université de Kyoto.	Abschlus an der Universität von Kioto.
1964	Completes his studies at University of Tokyo.	Termine ses études à l'Université de Tokyo.	Beendet sein Studium an der Universität von Tokio.
1960	Co-founder of the Metabolist Group.	Cofondateur du Mouvement Métaboliste.	Mitbegründer der *Metabolista* –Gruppe.
1965	Takamura Kotaro Award.	Prix Takamura Kotaro.	Takamura Kotaro-Preis.
1986	Honorary Member of the *Royal Institute of British Architects*.	Membre honoraire du Royal Institute of British Architects.	Ehrenmitglied des *Royal Institute of British Architects*.
1989	*Chevalier de L'Ordre des Arts et des Lettres of Frances*.	Chevalier de l'Ordre des Arts et des Lettres, France.	*Chevalier de l'Ordre des Arts et des Lettres in Frankreich*.
1990	Award from the *Architectural Institute of Japan*.	Prix de l'Architectural Institute of Japan.	Preis des *Architectural Institute of Japan*.
1992	*Japan Art Academy* Prize.	Prix de la Japan Art Academy.	Preis der *Japan Art Academy*.

WAKAYAMA MUSEUM

1994. Wakayama, Japan.

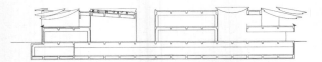

This museum is located very near the Wakayama castle, in the gardens that surround it, and now divided into two areas. The project consists of two buildings: the larger one houses the exhibitions of modern international art, both temporary and permanent ones; the smaller one holds exhibitions of regional-local interest. The architecture of this museum is permeable to the traditional Japanese forms. The complex relationship between interior and exterior is posed which in Japanese tradition receives the name of "engawa" and acquires the status of, not of limit, but rather, "intermediate space".

Ce musée se trouve près du château de Wakayama, dans les jardins qui l'entourent, aujourd'hui divisés en deux. Le projet est constitué de deux bâtiments: le plus grand héberge les expositions permanentes et temporaires d'art moderne international; le plus petit accueille les expositions régionales et locales. L'architecture du musée est perméable aux formes japonaises traditionnelles. Elle établit la relation complexe entre intérieur et extérieur, appelée "engawa" dans la tradition japonaise, et représente non une limite, mais un "espace intermédiaire".

Dieses Museum befindet sich nahe bei der Wakayama-Burg, in den Gärten, die es umrunden, und jetzt in zwei Areale unterteilt sind. Das Projekt ist aus zwei Gebäuden gebaut: Das größere beinhaltet internationale Austellungen moderner Kunst, sowohl permanente als auch temporäre; das kleinere nimmt Austellungen von regionalem lokalen Interesse auf. Die Architektur dieses Museums ist durchlässig für traditionelle japanische Formen. Es wird die komplexe Beziehung żwischen Innen und Außen angegangen, die in der japanischen Tradition den Namen "engawa" hat und nicht den limitierten Status erlangt, sondern den "mittleren Raum".

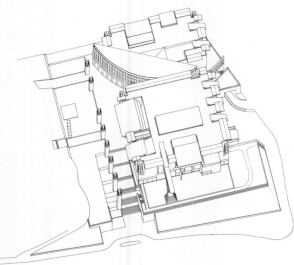

The facade, contrary to the interior, is not a continuous and smooth line, but rather, broken lines, clefts, and protrusions which makes it an expressive and articulate form.

Contrairement à l'intérieur, la façade n'est pas une ligne continue et lisse, mais présente des traits discontinus, des rainures et des saillies. C'est une forme articulée et expressive.

Die Fassade ist im Gegensatz zum Innenraum keine durchgehende und glatte Linie, sondern präsentiert unterbrochene Striche, Spalten und Vorsprünge, die sie in eine gegliederte und expresive Form verwandeln.

1995. Singapore.

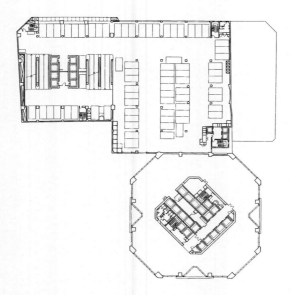

The perimeter of the base of the building could be defined as a square adjusted to the cardinal coordinates, whose four corners have been chamfered so that they almost form an octogan. The cardinal sides are always vertical planes whereas the diagonal sides (cants) slant progressively towards the interior, increasing the surface.

Le périmètre de la base de l'édifice pourrait être défini comme un carré ajusté aux points cardinaux, dont les quatre angles ont étés chanfreinés pour pratiquement former un octogone. Les faces cardinales gardent leur plan vertical, alors que les faces diagonales (plans coupés) s'inclinent progressivement vers l'intérieur, augmentant sa surface.

Der Umfang der Basis des Gebäudes könnte wie ein an die Hauptkoordinaten angepasstes Quadrat definiert werden, dessen vier Ecken gestreckt wurden, um fast ein Achteck zu bilden. Die Hauptseiten bleiben immer flache Vertikale, während die Diagonalen sich progressiv nach innen neigen und ihre Oberfläche vergrößern.

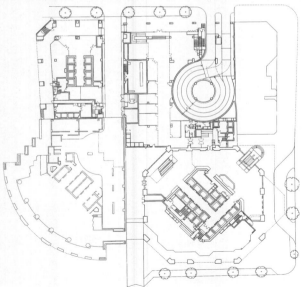

The main tower of 66 floors, is complemented with a low body consisting of a podium of five floors, designed for office use.

A la tour principale de 66 étages s'ajoute un corps bas de cinq étages destiné à une administration bancaire.

Der Hauptturm mit 66 Stockwerken wird von einem niedrigen Körper begleitet, der aus einem Podium mit fünf Stockwerken besteht, und für Büros von Banken vorgesehen ist.

Ricardo **Legorreta**

Ricardo Legorreta has created his own style by bringing elements of Mexican culture to contemporary architecture. What stands out in his works is the use of a wall as a construction structure and the combination of traditional colors with natural light in order to create geometric shapes that strike us as warm but at the same time, mysterious. The work of Legorreta in the U.S.A. shows an evolution of this style adapted to North American culture.

Ricardo Legorreta a créé un style propre en introduisant des éléments de la culture mexicaine dans l'architecture contemporaine. Ses œuvres se caractérisent par l'utilisation du mur comme structure constructive, et par la combinaison de couleurs traditionnelles à la lumière naturelle pour créer des formes géométriques à la fois accueillantes et mystérieuses. Les ouvrages de Legorreta aux Etats-Unis témoignent d'une évolution de ce style pour s'adapter à la culture du pays.

Ricardo Legorreta hat über die Elemente der mexikanischen Kultur zur zeitgenössischen Architektur einen eigenen Stil geschaffen. Seine Werke heben zum Beispiel die Mauer als konstruktive Struktur hervor und die Kombination von traditionellen Farben mit natürlichem Licht zur Schaffung geometrischer Formen, die gemütlich sind, gleichzeitig aber auch misteriös sein können. Die Arbeiten von Legorreta in den USA zeigen eine Entwicklung dieses Stils zur Anpassung an die nordamerikanische Kultur.

1931	Born in Mexico D.F., Mexico.	*Naît à Mexico, Mexique.*	Geboren in Mexiko Stadt, Mexiko.
1953	Degree in architecture from the Universidad Autonoma, Mexico.	*Diplôme d'architecte de l'Universidad Autónoma de México.*	Titel als Architekt von der *Universidad Autónoma de México.*
1963	Founds Legorreta Architects.	*Fonde Legorreta Arquitectos.*	Gründet *Legoretta Arquitectos.*
1970-71	Member of the *International Council of the Museum of Modern Art* in New York.	*Membre de l'*International Council of the Museum of Modern Art *de New York.*	Mitglied des *International Council of the Museum of Modern Art* in New York.
1981-94	Member of the jury of the Pritzker Prize.	*Membre du jury du Prix Pritzker.*	Mitglied der Jury für den Pritzker-Preis.
1992	National Fine Arts Award of Mexico.	*Prix National des Beaux Arts du Mexique.*	Nationalpreis der *Bellas Artes* in Mexiko.
1999	Gold Medal from the *International Union of Architects.*	*Médaille d'Or de l'*International Union of Architects.	Goldmedallie der *International Union of Architects.*
2000	Gold Medal from the *American Institute of Architects.*	*Médaille d'Or de l'*American Institute of Architects.	Goldmedallie des *American Institute of Architects.*

1994. San Nicolás de los Ganza, Nuevo León, México.

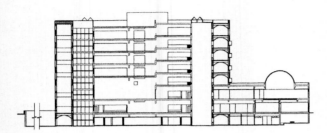

Located in the park of the "Children Heroes" in Monterrey, between the velo-drome of the city and a lake, the library had to not only satisfy the require-ments of an extensive program but also to respond adequately to a difficult situation on the edge of the lake. From the beginning, an attempt to inte-grate it with the landscape was sought by means of a volumetric composi-tion integrated with nature.
The principal body of the library is made up of two great volumes, a central cube inscribed in a cylinder which embraces it. The cylindrical crown opens towards the lake, finishing off in the shape of triangular pillars, of which the largest hangs over the water.

Située dans le parc des "Enfants Héros" de Monterrey, entre le vélodrome mu-nicipal et un lac, la bibliothèque devait non seulement remplir un lourd cahier des charges, mais également s'adapter à sa délicate situation près du lac. Dès le départ, l'architecte voulut intégrer l'œuvre à son environnement grâce à une composition volumétrique liée à la nature. Le corps principal de la biblio-thèque est constitué de deux grands volumes: un cube central inscrit dans un cylindre qui l'entoure. La couronne cylindrique s'ouvre face au lac, et s'achève en piédroits triangulaires, dont le plus grand se déverse directement sur l'eau.

Die Bibliothek, die sich im Park "Niños Héroes" in Monterrey zwischen dem Velodrom der Stadt und einem See befindet, sollte nicht nur die Vorraus-setzung für ein weitläufiges Programm sein, sondern auch adäquat die schwierige Lage am Ufer des Sees lösen. Von Anfang an suchte man eine Integration mit dem Umfeld über eine volumetrische Komposition, die mit der Natur in Verbindung steht. Der Hauptkörper der Bibliothek besteht aus zwei großen Gebäuden, einem zentralen Würfel, der sich in einen Zylinder einfügt, der ihn umarmt. Die zylinderförmige Krone öffnet sich in Richtung See in einer Dreiecksform, von denen sich die größte direkt über dem Wasser ausbreitet.

In spite of its great size, the macle of volumes fits into the surroundings, in an elegant scene with the lake and the park.

En dépit de ses dimensions impressionnantes, la macle de volumes s'intègre à son environnement dans une élégante étreinte avec le lac et le parc.

Wegen seiner Größe integriert sich die Macla der Außenansicht in einen eleganten Übergang mit dem See und dem Park in die Umgebung.

EDIFICIO DE OFICINAS EN MONTERREY

1995. Monterrey, Nuevo León, México.

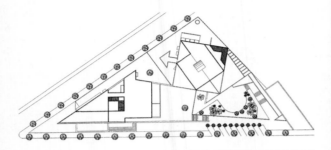

The project, located in a triangular lot in the Mexican city of Monterrey, needed a space for high-category offices. The client, a businessman who was the proprietor of a collection of contemporary Mexican art, needed his own place to work where, on the one hand, his own collection would fit, and on the other hand, be able to offer space for offices to rent. The color, like in all of Legorreta's work, has a special protagonism. Basically he differentiates the buildings by means of bright colors: orange for the offices and yellow for his private building.

Situé sur un terrain triangulaire de la ville mexicaine de Monterrey, le projet devait offrir un espace à de prestigieux bureaux. Le client, un homme d'affaires propriétaire d'une collection d'art contemporain mexicain, recherchait un lieu de travail et d'accueil pour sa collection, ainsi qu'un espace de bureaux à louer. Comme dans toutes les œuvres de Legorreta, la couleur joue un rôle particulier. Il choisit de différencier les bâtiments par des couleurs vives: orange pour les bureaux, et jaune pour le bâtiment privé.

Das Projekt welches sich auf einem dreiecksförmigen Grundstück in der mexikanischen Stadt Monterrey befindet, war für exklusive Büroräume bestimmt. Der Kunde, ein Geschäftsmann und Besitzer einer Sammlung zeitgenössischer mexikanischer Kunst, brauchte einen eigenen Ort zum Arbeiten, der einserseits auch Platz für seine Sammlung bietet, und andererseits Büroräume zum vermieten bietet.Die Farbe spielt, wie im gesamten Werk von Legorreta, eine besondere Rolle. Im Prinzip unterscheidet er die Gebäude durch zwei lebendige Farben: Orange für die Büros und gelb für private Gebäude.

The numerous works of contemporary art are integrated into a pleasant atmosphere, unusual in an office building, where the ground floor is an authentic art gallery.

Les nombreuses œuvres d'art contemporain s'intègrent dans une atmosphère agréable, inhabituelle dans un ensemble de bureaux. Le rez-de-chaussée est une véritable galerie d'art.

Die zahlreichen Werke zeitgenössischer Kunst integrieren sich in eine angenehme Atmosphäre, was ungewöhnlich für ein Bürogebäude ist; das Erdgeschoß ist eine echte Kunstgalerie.

1995. San Antonio, Texas, U.S.A.

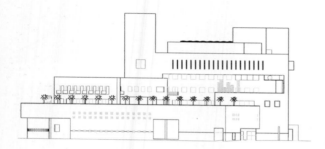

In this case, Legorreta Architects have bet on the singular character of a unique building in the center district of the city of San Antonio. A focal point of an anodyne urban setting, an architecture that gets dressed for a party, is charged with colors and presents its best shows to the city by means of the multiplicity of volumes and spaces that it contains.

Pour cette réalisation, Legorreta Arquitectos a opté pour le caractère singulier d'un bâtiment unique dans le centre-ville de San Antonio. Point focal au milieu d'un paysage urbain anodin, son architecture revêt un air de fête, se pare de couleurs, et présente son plus beau spectacle à la ville par la multiplicité de ses volumes et espaces.

In diesem Fall hat *Legorreta Architectos* um den einzigartigen Charakter eines einzigartigen Gebäudes im Zentrum von San Antonio gewettet. Ein fokaler Punkt in einer faden urbanen Landschaft, eine Architektur, die sich als Fest sieht, mit einer schweren Farbgebung und die der Stadt ihre besten Kleider über die Vielfalt der Gebäude und Zwischenräume präsentiert.

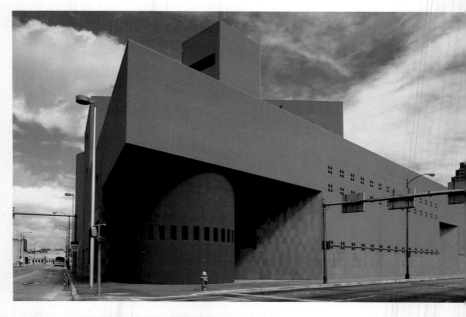

The principal volume rises six floor
above ground level and has a grea
atrium with zenithal illuminatio
all along the top. This central bod
experiences continual volumetri
variations because of the hollow
on its sides.

Le volume principal de six étage
renferme un vaste atrium, envah
dans toute sa hauteur par la lumiè
re zénithale. Chaque face de ce corp
central, par ses ouvertures, subit d
nombreuses variations volumé
triques.

Das Hauptgebäude hebt 6 Stokkwerke aus dem Boden und hat ei
zenital beleuchtetes Atrium übe
die ganze Höhe. Dieser zentrale Kör
per erlebt konstante volumetrisch
Variationen über die Leere in sei
nem Gesicht.

Mecanoo

In some ways we could say that the work of Mecanoo is "post-modernist" in that it uses past models to emphasize them in present-day architecture. Nevertheless, in this re-utilization of history the virtuosity of the team is demonstrated: once chosen the path to develop, they go in depth with construction methods with special care given to details. Through this process they have even gone so far as to experiment with the ways to standardization.

L'œuvre de Mecanoo pourrait en quelque sorte être qualifiée de "postmoderniste", en cela qu'elle utilise des modèles du passé pour les intégrer à l'architecture actuelle. Cette réutilisation de l'histoire n'entache cependant en rien tout le virtuose de l'équipe: une fois la démarche définie, ils élaborent des méthodes de construction en portant une attention particulière aux détails. Ce processus les mena même à expérimenter la voie de la standardisation.

In gewissem Sinne können wir sagen, das das Werk von Mecanoo "postmodern" ist während sie Modelle aus der Vergangenheit zu ihrer Betonung in der aktuellen Architektur verwenden. Ohne Zweifel manifestiert sich in dieser Wiederverwendung der Geschichte die Virtuosität des Teams: Einmal den Weg der Entwicklung gewählt, vertiefen sie die Konstruktionsmethoden mit einem Blick für ds Detail. Für diesen Prozeß haben sie sogar den Weg der Standardisierung ausprobiert.

	Henk Döll and Francine Houben were born in The Netherlands in 1956 and 1955, respectively.	Henk Döll et Francine Houben naissent aux Pays-Bas respectivement en 1956 et 1955.	Henk Döll und Francine Houben sind 1956 und 1955 in den Niederlanden geboren.
1984	Döll and Houben graduate from the *Technical University of Delft*.	*Obtiennent le diplôme de la* Technical University *de Delft*.	Machen ihren Abschluß and der *Technical University* von Delft.
1984	Founded the *Mecanoo Architecten* studio in Delft, The Netherlands.	*Fondent l'agence* Mecanoo Architecten *à Delft, Pays-Bas*.	Gründung des Büros *Mecanoo Architecten* in Delft, Niederlande.
2000	Award from the *4ª Bienal Internacional de Arquitetura*, in Sao Paolo, Brazil.	*Prix de la 4ª Bienal Internacional de Arquitetura, Sao Paolo, Brésil*.	Preis der 4. *Bienal Internacional de Arquitetura* in Sao Paolo, Brasilien.

1994. Maastricht, The Netherlands.

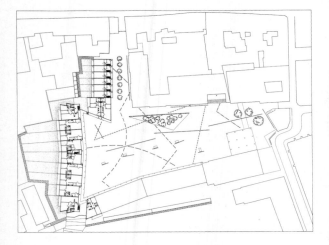

The plaza over which this dwelling was built was an interior patio with farms and small businesses. The architects attempted to recuperate this intimate character in a new plaza, public this time. A perimetral portico paved with quartzite was built that delimited the public and private space. The dwellings are situated behind a varnished cedar screen which hides the living rooms, balconies and back porches. A gallery connects the two blocks creating the illusion of one sole facade.

La place où furent construites ces habitations était une cour intérieure avec des fermes et des petits commerces. Les architectes ont voulu reproduire cette intimité dans une nouvelle place, publique cette fois-ci. Un porche pavé de quartzite la délimite, et sépare espace public et espace privé. Les salles de séjour, balcons et galeries des habitations sont protégés par un panneau en cèdre vernis. Une galerie relie les deux blocs, créant ainsi une impression de façade unique.

Der Platz, über dem dieses Wohnhaus gebaut wurde, war ein Innenhof mit kleinen Bauernhöfen und kleinen Geschäften. Die Architekten wollten diesen intimen Charakter auf einem neuen Platz wiederbeleben, diesmal öffentlich. Man baute ein umfangreiches Portal, belegt mit quartz, welches eine Trennung zwischen öffentlichen und privatem Raum schaffte. Die Wohnungen befinden sich hinter einer Wand aus lackiertem Zedernholz, die die Wohnzimmer, Balkone und Galerien verdeckt. Eine Galerie verbindet die beiden Blöcke und schafft so die Illusion einer einzigen Fassade.

FACULTY OF ECONOMICS AND MANAGEMENT

1995. Utrecht, The Netherlands.

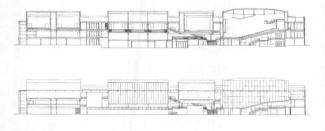

The faculty of Economics of the Polytechnic of Utrecht is located in a zone of the campus "de Uithof" called the kasbah. The urban development of this zone of the campus is characterized by its compressibility, by the low height of the buildings and its introspection, developed around interior patios. The more than 23.000 square meters of this center are developed, likewise, around three patios in only three floors.

La faculté d'Economie de l'Ecole Polytechnique d'Utrecht se trouve dans une zone du campus "de Uithof" appelée la casbah. L'essor urbain de cette partie du campus se caractérise par sa compacité, la faible hauteur de ses bâtiments, et son introspection, résultat de son organisation autour de cours intérieures. De la même manière, les plus de 23.000 m² de ce centre évoluent autour de trois cours, et sur seulement trois étages.

Die Fakultät für Wirtschaft der Polytechnischen Universität von Utrecht befindet sich in einer Zone des Campus "de Uithof" der auch als Kaspah bezeichnet wird. Die urbane Entwicklung dieser Zone des Campus zeichnet sich durch seine Kompaktheit aus, die geringe Höhe der Gebäude und ihrer Introspektive, die sich rund um die Innenhöfe entwickelt. Die mehr als 23000 m² dieses Zentrums entwickeln sich auch rund um die drei Innenhöfe auf nur drei Etagen.

Exterior catwalks roam among bamboo, connecting the different related spaces around the patio on the first floor.

Au premier étage, des passerelles extérieures traversent les bambous, et relient les divers espaces de rencontre autour de la cour.

Die Außenbrücken verlaufen zwischen Bambus und verbinden die verschiedenen Plätze rund um den Innenhof auf der ersten Etage.

Rafael **Moneo**

L'ILLA DIAGONAL

STOCKHOLM MUSEUM OF MODERN ART

Each of the projects realized by Moneo is posed as a theme of reflection, whether it be on the city, the topography, classical language or traditional typologies. No building of Moneo is the same as another. Navarro the architect distrusts the style oddities "I would like to not fall into the ridiculous trap of linguistic mistakes, this sensation that we have when we contemplate some of the recent architecture, destroyed by the attempt to identify paradigms, ignoring the real problems.

Chaque projet de Moneo se pose comme un sujet de réflexion, que ce soit sur la ville, la topographie, le langage classique, ou les typologies traditionnelles. Chacune de ses œuvres est différente. Cet architecte navarrais se méfie des figures de style: "j'aimerais éviter de tomber dans le ridicule de l'évocation linguistique, cette impression que l'on a souvent à contempler certaines architectures récentes, anéanties par l'intention d'appliquer des paradigmes, en passant à côté des vrais problèmes".

Jedes von Moneo realisierte Projek wird wirals ein Thema zum Nachden ken betrachtet, sei es über die Stadt, di Topographie, die klassische Sprach oder die traditionellen Typologien. Kein Gebäude Moneos ist wie das ander Der Architekt aus Navarra misstrau den Ticks der Stile."Ich möchte nicht fü einen linguistischen Irrtum ins Lächer liche gezogen werden, diesen Eindruck den wir oft haben, wenn wir einige der jüngsten Architekturen betrachten, di durch die Absicht, Paradigmen zu iden tifizieren, zerstört werden und die wirk lichen Probleme vergessen."

1937	Born in Tudela, Navarra, Spain.	*Naît à Tudela, Navarre, Espagne.*	Geboren in Tudela, Navarra, España.
1961	Completes his studies at the Escuela Superior de Arquitectura in Madrid.	*Termine ses études à l'Escuela Técnica Superior de Arquitectura de Madrid.*	Beendet sein Studium an der *Escuela Técnica Superior de Arquitectura* in Barcelona.
1970-80	Professorship of Composition Elements at the Escuela Tecnica Superior de Arquitectura in Barcelona.	*Chaire d'Eléments de Composition de l'Escuela Técnica Superior de Arquitectura de Barcelone.*	Dozent für Zusammengesetzte Elemente *Escuela Técnica Superior de Arquitectura* in Barcelona
1985	Named dean of the Graduate School of Design of the University of Harvard.	*Nommé doyen de la Graduate School of Design de l'Université d'Harvard.*	Nominiert zum Dekan der *Graduate School of Design* der *Havard University.*
1992	Gold Medal of Merit of the Fine Arts of the Government of Spain.	*Médaille d'Or du Mérite des Beaux Arts du Gouvernement espagnol.*	Goldmedallie *Mérito de las Bellas Artes* der spanischen Regierung.
1993	Arnold W. Brunner Award from the *American Academy and Institute of Arts and Letters.*	*Prix Arnold W. Brunner de l'American Academy and Institute of Arts and Letters.*	Arnold W. Brunner-Preis der *American Academy and Institute of Arts and Letters.*
1996	Pritzker Prize of architecture.	*Prix Pritzker d'Architecture.*	Pritzker-Preis für Architektur
1996	Gold Medal from the *International Union of Architects.*	*Médaille d'Or de l'International Union of Architects.*	Goldmedallie der *International Union of Architects.*

L'Illa Diagonal

1997. Barcelona, España.

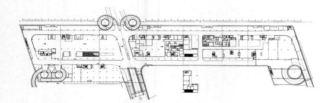

The play of shapes that the architects design in this project – where very diverse uses and activities are integrated – are not meant to produce an architectural image, but rather, urbanistic, as if it were a piece of the city. The facade evokes a set of buildings of different heights and the upper floors are set back from the plane of the facade.

Dans ce projet aux divers usages et activités, les architectes utilisent un jeu de formes dont le but n'est pas de créer une image architectonique, mais urbanistique, comme s'il s'agissait d'un bout de ville. La façade évoque un ensemble d'immeubles de hauteurs différentes, et les étages supérieurs sont en retrait par rapport au plan de cette façade.

Das Formenspiel, das die Architekten in dieses Projekt einbezogen haben –in das sich ein sehr unterschiedlicher Gebrauch und unterschiedliche Aktivitäten integrieren– soll kein architektonisches Bild produzieren, sondern ein urbanistisches, als wäre es ein Stück der Stadt. Die Fassade vermittelt einen Gebäudekomplex mit unterschiedlichen Höhen und die oberen Stockwerke liegen weiter hinter der Fassade.

The volumetric differences are shown by the variations of the effects of the sun, by the shadows that are projected.

Les différences volumétriques sont marquées par les variations des reflets du soleil et les ombres projetées.

Die verschiedenen Volumetrien zeigen sich durch die Variationen des Sonneneinfalls und den Schatten, die sie projezieren.

In this project, public and private interests are integrated, in such a way that next to the floors of offices and commercial surfaces buildings of cultural character have been incorporated.

Ce projet conjugue intérêts publics et privés. Aux bureaux et espaces commerciaux s'ajoutent des espaces culturels.

In dieses Projekt sind öffentliche und private Interessen eingeflossen, so, daß an die Büro- und Geschäftsetagen Gebäude mit kulturellem Charakter angeschlossen sind.

Stockholm Museum of Modern Art

1998. Stockholm, Sweden.

The project is based on the typological study of exhibition halls. Moneo has chosen to build halls with square floor plans and pyramidal roofs, finished off with a central skylight. Each hall has its own independent roof. One of the other important elements of the museum is the great glassed terrace of the cafeteria.

Le projet repose sur l'étude typologique des salles d'exposition. Moneo opta pour des salles carrées, et des toitures pyramidales coiffées d'une lucarne centrale. Chaque salle a un toit indépendant. Autre élément important du musée, la grande terrasse vitrée de la cafétéria.

Das Projekt basiert auf der typoligischen Studie der Ausstellungsräume. Moneo war der Meinung, einige quadratische und pyramidenförmig überdachte Ausstellungssäle zu konstruieren, die in einer zentralen Dachluke enden. Jeder Saal hat ein unabhängiges Dach. Ein anderes wichtiges Element des Museums ist die verglaste Terasse der Cafeteria.

The volumetry at the street shows a parallel line to this, generating the principal facade of the complex, whereas the posterior one is organized from volumes spaced out which are set back from the line of the facade.

La volumétrie frontale dessine une ligne parallèle à la rue, et forme la façade principale de l'ensemble. La volumétrie arrière est constituée de volumes échelonnés qui se retranchent par rapport à la ligne de façade.

Die Volumetrie zur Straße beschreibt ein parallele Line zu dieser, die die Hauptfassade des Komplexes generiert, während die vorige sich nach den abgestuften Gebäuden richtet, die sich hinsichtlich der Fassadenlinie wieder beruhigen.

Jean **Nouvel**

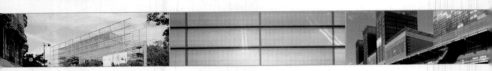

Until the beginning of the eighties, the position of Jean Nouvel was eclectic but with a common thread running through it: criticism and a frontal attack on the preestablished values of classical and modern architecture, and on the legal and monopolizing anachronism of the administrative bureaucracy.

For Jean Nouvel, architecture must allow the crystallization of the spirit of your time and provoke the spatial consolidation of a culture and of an imaginary.

Jusqu'au début des années quatre-vingt, la position de Jean Nouvel fut éclectique, bien qu'ayant une constante: une bataille ouverte contre les valeurs préétablies de l'architecture classique et moderne, et contre l'anachronisme légal et monopolisateur de la bureaucratie administrative. Pour Jean Nouvel, l'architecture doit permettre la cristallisation de l'esprit de son époque, et provoquer la consolidation spatiale d'une culture et d'un imaginaire.

Bis Anfang der 8oer war die Position von Jean Nouvel eklektisch, aber mit einer Konstante: Die Kritik und frontale Attacke gegen die vorentwickelten Werte der klassischen und modernen Architektur und gegen den legalen Anachronismus und der Monopolisierung der administrativen Bürokratie. Für Jean Nouvel muß die Architektur ein Kristallisierung des Geistes seiner Epoche erlauben und die räumliche Konsolidierung einer Kultur und einer Vorstellung provozieren.

1945	Born in fumel, France.	*Naît à Fumel, France.*	Geboren in Fumel, Frankreich.
1972	Degree in architecture from the *École National Supérior des Beaux Arts.*	*Licence d'architecture de l'École Nationale Supérieure des Beaux Arts.*	Diplom in Architektur an der École National Supérieur des Beaux Arts.
1987	Founds the *Jean Nouvel et Emmanuel Catan* studio.	*Fonde l'agence* Jean Nouvel et Emmanuel Catan.	gründet das Büro *Jean Nouvel und Emmanuel Catan.*
1989	*Gran Prix National d'Architecture* of France.	*Grand Prix National d'Architecture de France.*	*Gran Prix National d'Architecture* in Frankreich.
1995	Founds the *Architectures Jean Nouvel* studio.	*Fonde l'agence* Architectures Jean Nouvel.	Gründet das Büro *Architectures Jean Nouvel.*
1995	Honorary Member of the *Royal Institute of British Architects.*	*Membre honoraire du* Royal Institute of British Architects.	Ehrenmitglied des *Royal Institute of British Architects.*
1999	Gold Medal from the *l'Académie FranÇaise d'Architecture.*	*Médaille d'Or de l'Académie Française d'Architecture.*	Goldmedallie der *l'Académie Française d'Architecture.*
2001	The Francesco Borromini International Architecture Prize	*Prix International d'Architecture Francesco Borromini.*	Internationaler Architektur-Preis Francesco Borromini.

Fondation Cartier pour l'Art Contemporain

1994. Paris, France.

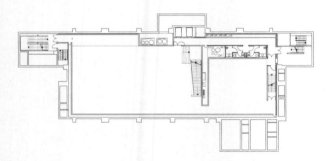

The Cartier Foundation is located at 261 Raspail Boulevard in Paris, in a small park which breaks the alignment of the one-floor dwellings along the street there. It consists of four floors and a mansard roof which are typical of the French capital. All the elements can be read like an articulated transparency by means of a series of parallel planes among themselves and to the line of Raspail Boulevard, among which the project is defined.

La Fondation Cartier se trouve au 261 du Boulevard Raspail à Paris, dans un petit parc qui casse l'alignement des immeubles d'habitations mansardés à quatre étages, typiques de la capitale française. Le projet se définit à travers une série de plans parallèles entre eux, et parallèles au Boulevard Raspail, articulant une transparence des éléments.

Die Cartier-Stiftung im 261. Pariser Boulevard Raspail, unterbricht in einem kleinen Park die Aufreihung der eingeschoßigen Wohnhäuser, vier Wohnungen in einem Block, typisch für die französische Hauptstadt. Alle Elemente lesen sich wie eine artikulierte Transparenz über eine Reihe von Ebenen parrallel zum Boulevard Raspail, zwischen denen sich das Projekt befindet.

The trees have a protagonistic role in the configuration of the building.

Les arbres ont un rôle défini dans la configuration du bâtiment.

Die Bäume spielen eine protagonistische Rolle in der Konfiguration des Gebäudes.

In the interior the same materials predominate as in the exterior: glass and lacquered metal in gray tones.

A l'intérieur, prédominent les mêmes matériaux qu'à l'extérieur: verre et métal laqué dans des tons gris.

Im Inneren dominieren die gleichen Materialien wie außen: Glas und graulakiertes Metall.

From the boulevard, the building becomes a halo which envelops the trees and changes them into virtual objects.

Depuis le boulevard, le bâtiment devient un halo enveloppant les arbres et les dédoublant en objets virtuels.

Vom Boulevard aus verwandelt sich das Gebäude in einen Halo, der die Bäume mitreißt und sie in virtuelle Objekte kopiert.

Triangle des Gares. Euralille

1994. Lille, France.

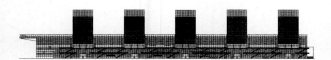

Situated at the confluence of the line of the High-Speed Train from Paris to London, there is the Triangle des Gares, an extensive commercial center crowned by a row of office towers to the south, and bordered by a front of dwellings and a hotel to the west. The center groups a crucible of activities and functions at a site conceived as a crossroads of comings and goings. The lacquered aluminum provides the building with a gray background, and it constitutes a graphic support on which sets of advertisement, logotypes, reflective paint and intense red lights that introduce into the building the aesthetics of an airport, motorways, television or the screen of a computer, not as a metaphor, but rather as the acceptation and the staging of the image of the present-day world.

Le Triangle des Gares est un immense centre commercial couronné d'une rangée de tour de bureaux au sud, et bordé d'un ensemble d'habitations et d'un hôtel à l'ouest. Il se trouve sur la ligne TGV Paris-Londres. Le centre réunit une pléiade d'activités et de fonctions dans un environnement conçu comme un carrefour de déplacements et de fluences. L'aluminium laqué donne au bâtiment un fond gris neutre, et représente un support graphique pour les publicités, logotypes, peintures réfléchissantes et lumières d'un rouge intense, qui introduisent dans le bâtiment l'esthétique des aéroports, autoroutes, télévision ou écran d'ordinateur, non comme métaphore, mais comme acceptation et mise en scène de l'image du monde actuel.

Das *Triangle des Gares*, ein weitläufiges Einkaufszentrum, das im Süden von einer Reihe von Bürotürmen gekrönt und im Osten an eine Front aus Wohnhäusern und ein Hotel angrenzt, befindet sich im Zusammenfluß mit der Bahntrasse des französischen Hochgeschwindigkeitszuges TGV Paris-London. Das Zentrum vereint einen Schmelztiegel von Aktivitäten und Funktionen in einer Umgebung, die wie eine Kreuzung von Deplazierungen und Flüssen gesehen werden muß. Das lackierte Aluminium verleiht dem Gebäude einen neutralen grauen Hintergrund, und konstituiert eine graphische Unterstützung, über die sich Annoncenspiele, Logotypen, reflektierende Gemälde und intensiv rote Lichter auseinanderbreiten, die das Gebäude in die Ästhetik von Flughäfen, Autobahnen, Fernsehen oder dem Computerbildschirm nicht wie eine Metapher, sondern wie die Aktzeptanz und Inszenierung des aktuellen Weltbildes einführen.

The building of Lille plays with the superposition of two architectures: one which encloses the space and the other which provokes an image created by the logotypes of the companies that occupy the buildings.

Ce bâtiment de Lille joue avec la superposition de deux architectures: une qui enferme l'espace, et une autre qui provoque une image virtuelle à partir des logotypes des entreprises du centre.

Das Gebäude von Lille spielt mit der Überblendung zweier Architekturen: Einer, die den Raum einschließt, und eine andere, die ein Bild provoziert, daß von den Logos der ansässigen Firmen provoziert wird.

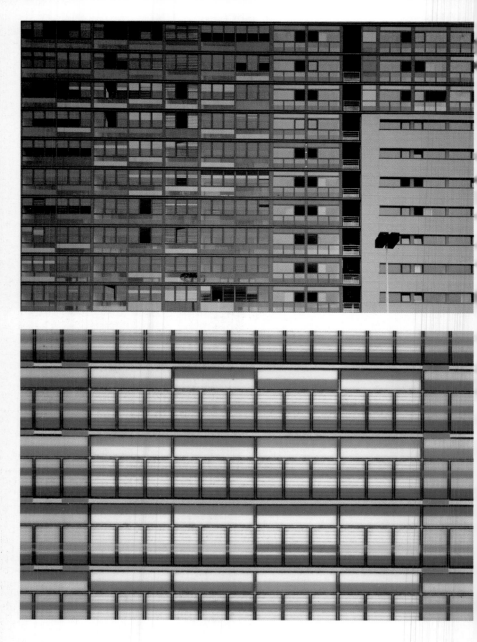

Eric **Owen Moss**

THE BOX
RESIDENCE LAWSON

In the work of Moss, the concept of mutability is the starting point of his research. Within the visual culture of constructivism and the tradition of Frank O. Gehry, his projects propose a new focus by means of the reformulation of the principles of architecture.

Dans l'œuvre de Moss, le concept de mutabilité est le point de départ de ses recherches. Au sein de la culture visuelle du constructivisme, et de la tradition de Frank O. Gehry, ses projets proposent une optique nouvelle, à travers la reformulation des principes architectoniques.

In dem Werk von Moss bildet das Konzept der Wechselhaftigkeit den Ausgangspunkt seiner Forschung. Innerhalb der visuellen Kultur des Konstruktivismus und der Tradition von Frank O. Gehry zeigen seine Projekte einen neuen Standpunkt über die Neuformulierung der architektonischen Prinzipien.

1943	Born in Los Angeles, U.S.A.	*Naît à Los Angeles, Etats-Unis.*	Geboren in Los Angeles, USA.
1965	Degree in art from the University of California.	*Licence d'art de l'Université de Californie.*	Absolvent der Kunstwissenschaften, Universität von Kalifornien.
1972	Architecture degree from the *Graduate School of Design* of the University of Harvard.	*Diplôme d'architecte de la* Graduate School of Design *de l'Université d'Harvard.*	Titel als Architekt von der *Graduate School of Design* der Harvard Universität.
1973	Founds *Eric Owen Moss Architects.*	*Fonde* Eric Owen Moss Architects.	Gründet *Eric Owen Moss Architects.*
1996	Invited architec at the *Biennale d'Architettura* in Venice.	*Architecte invité à la* Biennale d'Architettura *de Venise.*	Einladung zur *Biennale d'Architettura* in Venedig.
1999	Architecture Award from the *American Academy of Arts and Letters.*	*Prix d'Architecture de l'*American Academy of Arts and Letters.	Architekturpreis der *American Academy of Arts and Letters.*
2001	Gold Medal from the *American Institute of Architects.*	*Médaille d'Or de l'*American Institute of Architects.	Goldmedallie des *American Institute of Architects.*
2001	Merit Award for Design, *American Institute of Architects.*	Merit Award for Design, American Institute of Architects.	Merit Award for Design, *American Institute of Architects.*

THE BOX

1994. Culver City, California, U.S.A.

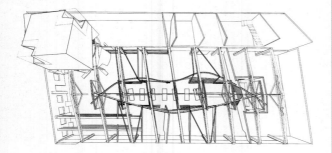

The box is an appendix of an old industrial building whose force comes from its plasticity, the fluence of shapes and from its implicit movement. Moss did not attempt to construct a space but rather, he proposes sensations, and experiments with sequences of images that have to be reelaborated in the mind of the visitor that passes through. The floor plan is rectangular and it has a structure of wooden ribs with a central pillar and a longitudinal lantern.

The Box est l'appendice d'une ancienne nef industrielle, qui tire sa force de sa plasticité, de la fluence des formes, et de son mouvement implicite. L'objectif de Moss n'était pas de construire un espace, mais de proposer des sensations, d'élaborer des séquences d'images que le visiteur doit reproduire dans son esprit. Le plan est rectangulaire, et la structure faite de cintres en bois, avec un pilier central et une lanterne longitudinale.

The Box ist der Anhang einer alten Industriehalle, dessen Kraft aus der Plastizität stammt, den fließenden Formen und deren impliziter Bewegungen. Moss hat nicht versucht eine Raum zu bauen, sondern er bietet Sensationen und experimentiert mit Bildsequenzen die im Verstand des Besuchers, der sie besichtigt wiederentwickelt werden müssen. Das Gebäude ist rechteckig und die Struktur besteht aus Holz mit einer zentralen Säule und einer länglichen Lampe.

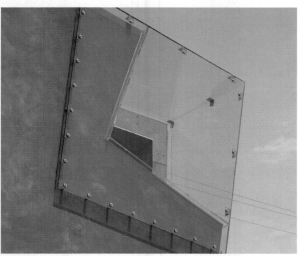

Conceptually it is a box with which things begin to occur: a slight inclination, the intersection with a cylinder on the ground floor, the formal vestige left behind from the way of ascension...

D'un point de vue conceptuel, c'est une boîte qui connaît des modifications: une légère inclinaison, l'intersection avec un cylindre au rez-de-chaussée, la piste formelle que laisse l'accès à l'étage...

Vom Begriff her ist es ein Kasten, in dem Dinge anfangen zu folgen: eine leichte Neigung, der Schnittpunkt mit einem Zylinder im Erdgeschoß, die formale Spur, die den eigenen Weg des Zogangs aufgibt.

Residence Lawson

1992. Brentwood, California, U.S.A.

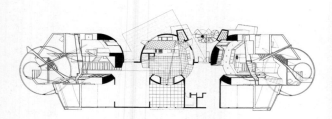

The formal language employed both in the interiors and on the facades comes from the application of some very concrete ideas in respect to the facts of domestics, with some ground-breaking results that, nevertheless, reflect the concern for detail and total design, in a conceptual dissection of the dwelling in all of its layers. Owen Moss does not limit himself to harmoniously ordering a series of conventional spaces, but rather, conceives architecture as a way to explore all the possibilities that any space can generate.

Le langage formel utilisé pour les intérieurs et les façades obéit à l'application d'idées très concrètes sur la vie domestique. L'effet est brise-tout, mais reflète une attention particulière au détail et à la conception d'ensemble, dans une dissection conceptuelle de l'habitation dans toutes ses strates. Owen Moss ne se limite pas à ordonner harmonieusement une série d'espaces conventionnels; il conçoit l'architecture comme une forme d'exploration de toutes les possibilités de chaque espace.

Die formale Sprache, die im Inneren ebenso angewendet wird wie in den Fassaden, verfolgt die Anwendung einiger sehr konkreter Ideen bezüglich der häuslichen Tatsache, mit einigen zerbrochenen Ergebnissen, die ohne Zweifel die Sorge um das Detail und den Gesamtentwurf reflektieren, in einer begrifflichen Sektion des Hauses in seiner ganzen Schicht. Owen Moss beschränkt sich nicht darauf, eine Reihe von konventionellen Räumen harmonisch anzuordnen, sondern er begreift die Architektur als eine Form, alle Möglichkeiten, die ein Raum generien kann, zu erforschen.

Marked by a great spatial ambiguity, the volume of the house stands out as the product of multiple geometric hybridizations, already perceptible from the planimetry.

Le volume de la maison est marqué par une grande ambiguïté spatiale, et apparaît comme le produit de multiples hybridations géométriques, perceptibles depuis la planimétrie.

Ausgezeichnet durch eine räumliche Zweideutigkeit, unterscheidet sich die Außenansicht des Hauses wie ein Produkt von mehreren geometrischen Hybridisierungen, die man schon von der Planimetrie her wahrnimmt.

Cesar **Pelli**

SEA HAWK HOTEL
PETRONAS TOWERS
NTT HEADQUARTERS BUILDING

The professional trajectory of this Argentine architect, established in the U.S.A., has developed above all, in the typology of skyscrapers. As a consequence, his buildings are an important part of the skyline of many cities. Pelli defines himself as a pragmatic architect. Therefore, his proposals are characterized by his following the indications that the project itself suggests, without confronting them with preconceived ideas.

La trajectoire professionnelle de cet architecte argentin basé aux Etats-Unis s'est avant tout développée au sein d'une typologie de gratte-ciel. Ses œuvres sont donc une partie importante de la ligne d'horizon de nombreuses villes. Pelli se définit comme un architecte pragmatique cherchant à suivre les indications du projet initial, sans l'interférence d'idées préconçues.

Der berufliche Werdegang diese argentinischen Architekten, der sich in den USA niedergelassen hat, hat sich vor allem in der Typologie der Wolkenkratzer entwickelt, in Konsequenz sind seine Gebäude wichtiger Bestandteil der Skyline in vielen Städten. Pelli definiert sich selbst als ein pragmatischer Architekt. Seine Vorschläge zeichnen sich dadurch aus, das er den Zeichen folgt, die das Projekt selbst anbietet, ohne sich ihnen mit vorgefassten Ideen gegenüberzustellen.

1926	Born in Tucumán, Argentina.	Naît à Tucuman, Argentine.	Geboren in Tucumán, Argentinien
1950	Degree in Architecture from the University of Tucumán.	Diplôme d'architecte de l'Université de Tucuman.	Abschluß als Architekt an der Universität von Tucumán.
1954	Master in the science of architecture from the University of Illinois.	Master en sciences de l'architecture de l'Université d'Illinois.	Master in Architekturwissenschaften an der Universität von Illinois.
1954-64	Works in the studio of Eero Saarinen.	Travaille pour l'agence de Eero Saarinen.	Arbeitet im *Büro Eero Saarinen*.
1977	Founds *Cesar Pelli & Associates*.	Fonde Cesar Pelli & Associates.	Gründet *Cesar Pelli & Associates*.
1977-84	Dean of the *School of Architecture* of the University of Yale.	Doyen de la School of Architecture de l'Université de Yale.	Dekan der *School of Architecture* der Univesität Yale.
1991	Chosen as one of the ten most influential living American Architects by the *American Institute of Architects*.	Sélectionné comme l'un des dix architectes américains vivants les plus influents par l'American Institute of Architects.	Augewählt vom *American Institute of Architects* als einer der zehn lebenden einflußreichsten amerikanischen Architekten
1995	Gold Medal from the *American Institute of Architects*.	Médaille d'Or de l'American Institute of Architects.	Goldmedallie des *Armerican Institute of Architects*.

Sea Hawk Hotel

1995. Fukuoka, Japan.

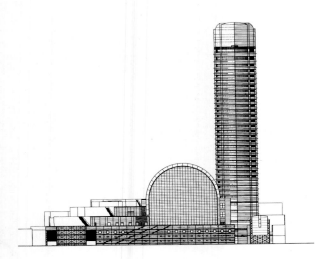

All of César Pelli's projects share a characteristic: the absence of preconceived ideas. Each project is designed in consonance with its individual context, that is to say, the place, the climate, and the culture. The design of this hotel, that springs forth from the earth like a lighthouse, creates in the bay a composition of sculptural shapes.

Tous les projets de César Pelli ont un point commun: l'absence d'idées préconçues. Chaque œuvre s'accorde à son contexte individuel, c'est-à-dire, le lieu, le climat et la culture. Le design de cet hôtel, qui surgit de la terre comme un phare, crée dans la baie une composition de formes structurales.

Alle Projekte von César Pelli haben eins gemeinsam: Das Fehlen von vorgefassten Ideen. Jedes Projekt ist in Übereinstimmung mit seinem individuellen Kontext entworfen worden, d. h. mit dem Ort, dem Klima und der Kultur. Der Entwurf dieses Hotels, das wie ein Leuchtturm aus der Erde ragt, schafft in der Meeresbucht eine Komposition aus bildhauerischen Formen.

The curves of the roof and the walls make reference to two of the elements that surround the building: air and water.

Les courbes du toit et des murs évoquent deux des éléments entourant le bâtiment: l'air et l'eau.

Die Rundungen des Daches und der Mauern beziehen sich auf zwei der Elemente, die das Gebäude umgeben: Luft und Wasser.

Petronas Towers

1997. Kuala Lumpur, Malaysia.

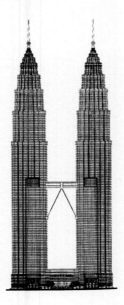

The initial condition of the project demanded that the towers would be Malayan. For this reason, the buildings were strongly linked to the conditions existing in the place and the culture of the country, from the first models. The most important project decision was to make the towers symetrical, entrusting to this fact, all the figurative and symbolic weight of the project. Between them, appears the void, an essential concept of asiatic cultures.

La première exigence du projet était d'ériger des tours malaises. Dès les premières ébauches, les bâtiments s'adaptent donc aux conditions environnementales et à la culture du pays. La décision la plus importante du projet fut de faire des tours symétriques, comptant ainsi sur l'impact figuratif et symbolique du projet. Entre les deux tours apparaît le vide, concept essentiel des cultures asiatiques.

Die Anfangskondition des Projekts machte es erforderlich, daß die Türme malaisisch wurden. Dafür beharren die Gebäude von der ersten Skizze an auf bestehenden Konditionen am Ort und der Landeskultur. Die wichtigste Entscheidung für das Projekt war, die Türme symetrisch zu bauen, und die gesamte darstellende und symbolische Last des Projektes dieser Tatsache anzuvertrauen. Zwischen ihnen taucht die Leere auf, ein essentielles Konzept der asiatischen Kulturen.

The axis of the complex is between the two towers, in the empty space. The power of this is increased by means of the pedestrian bridge that spans the two towers, where the lookout points over the city, are found.

L'axe de l'ensemble se place entre les deux tours, dans l'espace vide. La force de ce vide est incarnée par la passerelle piétonnière reliant les tours, d'où l'on peut admirer toute la ville.

Die Achse des Komplexes befindet sich zwischen den beiden Türmen, im leeren Raum. Die Kraft derselben vergrößert sich durch die Fußgängerbrücke, die die Türme verbindet, wo sich die Aussichtspunkte über die Stadt befinden.

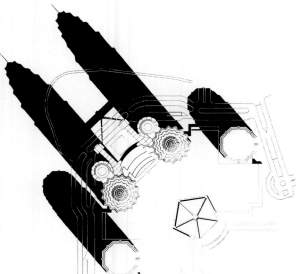

NTT Headquarters Building

1990-1995. Tokyo, Japan.

The tower is divided into two very clearly defined parts: a curved side that looks to the area of the garden where the offices are, and a triangular area with an exterior facade, where the areas of services and communications are located. The four metal parasols that are to be found on each floor, reinforce the image of an incomplete facade.

La tour se divise en deux parties bien distinctes: un côté courbé donnant sur les espaces verts où se trouvent les bureaux, et un espace triangulaire avec façade donnant sur l'extérieur, hébergeant les services et communications. Les quatre parasols métalliques de chaque plan renforcent l'image d'une façade incomplète.

Der Turm teilt sich in zwei gut definierte Teile: eine runde Seite, die bis zur Gartenzone geht, wo sich die Büros befinden, und ein dreieckiges Areal mit einer Aussenfassade, wo sich die Service- und Kommunikationszonen befinden. Die vier Sonnensschirme aus Metall, die sich in jedem Stockwerk befinden, vetstärken das Bild einer unvollständigen Fassade.

The building consists of three very differentiated parts: a thirty-storey tower, a lower body and a garden that connects them.

Le bâtiment est composé de trois parties bien distinctes: une tour de 30 étages, un corps inférieur, et un jardin qui les relie.

Das Gebäude besteht aus drei sehr verschiedenen Teilen: Ein 30stöckiger Turm, ein Innenkörper und ein Garten, der sie verbindet.

Dominique **Perrault**

Bibliothéque Nationale de France
Centre Technique du Livre Marne la Vallée

Although in the work of Perrault there is a great variety of textures, materials and colors, his buildings are characterized by the austerity in the volumetric proposal. Furthermore, he seeks a certain neutrality in the context. By means of the use of glass, transparencies and reflections are achieved that, on the one hand and during the day, tend to dissolve the volumes in the place, but on the other hand, during the night, converts them into authentic boxes of light.

Bien que l'œuvre de Perrault témoigne d'une grande variété de textures, matériaux et couleurs, ses bâtiments sont caractérisés par l'austérité de la volumétrie, et la recherche d'une relative neutralité dans le contexte. L'usage du verre permet des transparences et des reflets, qui à la fois dissolvent les volumes dans leur environnement le jour, et transforment ces volumes en véritables boîtes lumineuses la nuit.

Auch wenn in den Werken von Perrault eine große Vielfalt an Tetxturen, Materialien und Farben existiert, kennzeichen sich seine Gebäude durch die Nüchternheit in der Volumetrie, und außerdem durch die Suche nach Neutralität im Kontext. Über die Nutzung von Glas werden Transparenzen und Reflexe erreicht, die einerseits tagsüber die Auflösung der Außenansicht am Ort erreichen, und sie andererseits nachts in wahre Lichtkästen verwandeln.

1953	Born in Clermont-Ferrand, France.	Naît à Clermont-Ferrand, France.	Geboren in Clermont-Ferrand, Frankreich.
1978	Graduates from the *Ecole Nationale Supérieure de Beaux-Arts* in Paris.	Diplômé de l'Ecole Nationale Supérieure des Beaux-Arts de Paris.	Abschluß an der *Ecole Nationale Supérieure des Beaux-Arts* in Paris.
1979	Certificate of advanced studies in urbanism from the *Ecole Nationale de Ponts et Chaussées* in Paris.	Certificat d'Etudes Supérieures d'Urbanisme de l'Ecole Nationale des Ponts et Chaussées, Paris.	Abschluß in Stadtplanung an der *Ecole Nationale des Ponts et Chaussées* in Paris.
1980	Diploma from the *Ecole des Hautes Etudes in Sciences Sociales*.	Diplôme de l'Ecole des Hautes Etudes en Sciences Sociales.	Diplom an der *Ecole des Hautes Etudes* in Sozialwissenschaften.
1981	Founds his own studio in Paris.	Fonde sa propre agence à Paris.	Gründet sein eigenes Büro in Paris.
1993	Receives the *Gran Prix National d'Architecture* of France.	Grand Prix National d'Architecture de France.	*Gran Prix National d'Architecture* in Frankreich.
1997	*Chevalier de la Legión d'Honneur* of France.	Chevalier de la Légion d'Honneur, France.	*Chevalier de la Legión d'Honneur* in Frankreich.
1997	The *Mies van der Rohe* European Award of architecture.	Prix européen d'architecture Mies van der Rohe.	Europapreis für Architektur *Mies van der Rohe*.

Bibliothèque Nationale de France

1997. Paris, France.

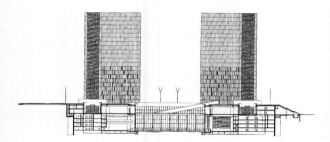

In this work the architect expresses two apparently opposing dimensions: the monumentality of the building symbolized by the towers, and a more intimate and humanized space where the reader can feel to be in an atmosphere which is nearer to him. This intention can be observed in the great expanse of wood over the podium, or in the use of materials such as wood or others which reflect the passing of time –red carpeting on the floors or metalic, achromatic fabrics–. The central garden can be seen as the soul of the project as it gives serenity to the complex.

L'architecte exprime dans cette œuvre deux dimensions apparemment opposées: la monumentalité du bâtiment, symbolisée par les tours, et un espace plus intime et humanisé, où le lecteur peut trouver un environnement plus proche. Cette volonté se reflète dans la vaste esplanade de bois sur le podium, ou dans l'usage de matériaux parmi lesquels le bois, les moquettes rouges ou les tissus métalliques en acier mate qui témoignent du passage du temps. Le jardin central incarne l'âme du projet, donne à l'ensemble toute sa sérénité.

Der Architekt drückt in diesem Werk zwei scheinbar gegensätzliche Dimensionen aus: Die Monumentalität des Gebäudes, die durch die Türme symbolisiert wird, und ein intimerer und humanisierter Platz, wo der Leser sich in einem nahen Ambiente setzen kann. Diese Absicht kann man auf dem großen freien Gelände mit Holz auf dem Podium, oder bei den Materialien, wie Holz und andere, die die Vergänglichkeit bezeugen, rotem Teppichboden oder den matten Metalldächern, beobachten. Der zentrale Garten ist wie die Seele des Projektes, er gibt dem Komplex Ruhe.

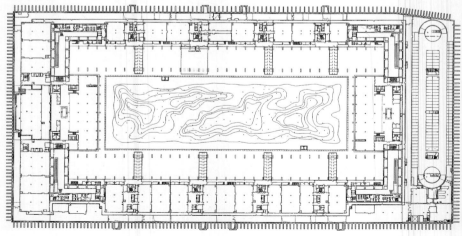

Four glass towers with shelves for books outline the brackets of an immense rectangular podium and outline a spatial hollow.

Quatre tours de verre, meublées d'étagères pour les livres, délimitent les angles d'un immense podium rectangulaire et encadrent un espace libre.

Vier Glastürme mit Bücherregalen limitieren die Dreiecke eines riesigen rechteckigen Podiums und rahmen einen Hohlraum ein.

Perrault situates the book deposit in the highest floors from where you can have the best views and the reading rooms on the lower floors.

Perrault place les salles de lecture dans les étages inférieurs, et le stockage des livres dans les étages supérieurs, d'où l'on peut jouir de l'une des plus belles vues de la ville.

Perrault platziert das Buchlager auf den höchsten Stockwerken, von wo man die besten Aussichten hat und die Lesesäle im Inneren.

An exhibition center, an auditorium, conference rooms and restaurants increase the public dimension of the library which also functions as the computerized center of French libraries.

Un centre d'exposition, un auditorium, des salles de conférence et des restaurants élargissent la dimension publique de la bibliothèque, qui fait également office de centrale d'un réseau informatisé des bibliothèques de France.

Ein Ausstellungszentrum, ein Auditorium, Konferenzsäle und Restaurants steigern die öffentliche Dimension der Bibliothek, die auch als Zentrale für ein Informationsnetzwerk französischer Bibliotheken dient.

Centre Technique du Livre Marne la Vallée

1995. Bussy-Saint-Georges, France.

In regards to the formal planning, the compositive axis of the ground plan is a covered, interior path, which organizes the distribution and communication between the diverse areas of the center. On one side of this path, like the teeth of a comb, perpendicular to it, you find the buildings that contain the workshops, offices, reading rooms and training rooms.

L'ordonnance du bâtiment repose sur un axe formé par une avenue intérieure couverte, qui organise la distribution et la communication des divers espaces du centre. Perpendiculaires à cette avenue, telles des dents de peigne, se trouvent les bâtiments des ateliers, bureaux, salles de conférence et de formation.

Bezüglich der formellen Ordnung ist die zusammengesetze Achse der Etage ein überdachter Weg, der die Verteilung und die Kommunikation zwischen den diversen Arealen des Zentrums organisiert. Auf deiner Seite dieses Weges, haben sich die Gebäude mit den Werkstätten, Büros, Konferenzsälen und Ausbildungsräumen angeordnet wie die senkrechten Zinken eines Kamms.

Antoine **Predock**

MESA PUBLIC LIBRARY

This architect attempts to reflect in his work the "inspiration" that each place gives in order to develop each project. A product of this search is that his architecture is charged with a mystical aura which reminds you of the conceptions of many of the masters of architecture. To this can be added the work of the project as a "choreographic event" which leads him to use multiple volumes, almost all simple, which become an important part of the landscape where it is set.

Pour l'élaboration de chacun de ses projets, cet architecte cherche à refléter dans son œuvre l'"inspiration" puisée dans le lieu. Produit de cette quête, son architecture est chargée d'une aura mystique rappelant les conceptions de nombreux maîtres de l'architecture. A cela s'ajoute un travail traité comme un "événement chorégraphique", qui le mène parfois à utiliser des volumes multiples, pour la majorité simples, et qui prennent de l'importance dans le paysage qui les accueille.

Dieser Architekt will in seinem Werk die "Inspiration" suchen, die ihm den Platz für die Entwicklung jedes Projekts gibt. Als Ergebnis dieser Suche hat seine Architektur eine mystische Aura, die an die Konzepte vieler Meister der Architektur erinnert. Damit vereint sich die Arbeit des Projekts wie ein "korreographisches Ereignis", die ihn in einigen Fällen zur Nutzung multipler Außenansichten bringt, fast alle einfach, sie verwandeln sich in einen wichtigen Teil der Landschaft, wo sie plaziert sind.

1936	Born in Lebanon, Missouri, U.S.A..	*Naît à Lebanon, Missouri, Etats-Unis.*	Geboren in Lebanon, Missouri, USA.
1962	Degree in architecture from the University of Columbia, after having studied at the University of New Mexico.	*Obtient le diplôme d'architecte de l'Université de Columbia, après avoir étudié à l'Université du Nouveau Mexique.*	Erhält seinen Architektentitel in der Universität von Columbia, nachdem er in der Universität von New Mexico studiert hat.
1985	Rome Award from the *American Academy* in Rome.	*Prix Rome de l'American Academy in Rome.*	Roma-Preis der *American Academy* in Rom.
1987	Sets up his own studio in Albuquerque.	*Ouvre sa propre agence à Albuquerque.*	Eröffnet sein eigenes Büro in Albuquerque.
1988	Opens an office in Los Angeles.	*Ouvre une filiale à Los Angeles.*	Eröffnet ein Büro in Los Angeles.
1989	Member of the *American Institute of Architects*.	*Membre de l'American Institute of Architects.*	Mitglied des *American Institute of Architects*.
1993	Prize from the *Albuquerque Chapter, American Institute of Architects*.	*Prix de l'Albuquerque Chapter de l'American Institute of Architects.*	*Albuquerque Chapter*-Preis des *American Institute of Architects*.

MESA PUBLIC LIBRARY

1994. Los Alamos, New Mexico, U.S.A.

The library can be situated halfway between sculptural abstraction and the integration into the natural context of the environs. The volume is a low body of two floors, cut in the center by a wedge of bigger height, which evokes the arrises of the rock walls of the region. At the intersection of the two elements, Predock projected a patio through which you can accede to the building.

La bibliothèque se trouve à mi-chemin entre l'abstraction sculpturale et l'intégration de l'œuvre à son environnement naturel. Son volume est composé d'un corps bas de deux étages, coupé en son centre par une cale plus haute, évoquant les arêtes des murs en pierres de la région. A l'intersection des deux éléments, Predock a placé un patio d'accès au bâtiment.

Die Bibliothek befindet sich auf halbem Weg zwischen bildhauerischer Abstraktion und der Integration in den natürlichen Kontext des Umfelds. Seine Außenansicht ist ein niedriger Körper mit zwei Etagen, die in der Mitte von einem hohen Keil durrchschnitten wird, der die Kanten der Felswände der Region heraufbeschwört. Im Schnittpunkt der zwei Elemente, hat Pedrock einen Innenhof entworfen, über den man das Gebäude betritt.

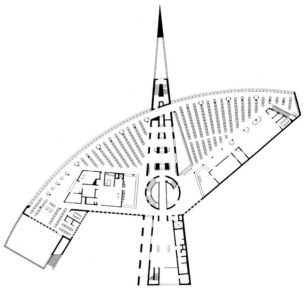

The principal material used is concrete, both in standard blocks and in poured shapes in situ, in the search for an analagous image to the monumental constructions of the primitive pueblos.

Le principal matériau utilisé est le béton, en bloc ou en parements coffrés in situ, dans l'intention d'obtenir une image analogue à celle des constructions gigantesques des peuples primitifs.

Das Hauptmaterial, das verwendet wird, ist Beton, sowohl in Blöcken als auch an Ort und Stelle gegossen, mit der Absicht, ein analoges Bild zu suchen, wie das der Monumentalbauten der primitiven Völker.

Søren **Robert Lund**

This Danish architect opened his own studio after winning the bid to construct the Arken Museum of Modern Art in Copenhagen, the project which put him into the international panorama. His works are expressed around metaphors which try to tell a story such as a shipwreck or the transformation of paper in a newspaper. Lund's designs search for the interaction with the environs, pay maximum attention to detail and utilize, preferably, basic materials.

Cet architecte danois ouvrit son propre cabinet lorsqu'il gagna le concours pour la construction du Musée Arken d'Art Moderne de Copenhague, projet qui lui apporta une reconnaissance mondiale. Ses œuvres s'articulent autour de métaphores racontant une histoire, celle d'un naufrage, ou de la métamorphose du papier en journal. Les projets de Lund recherchent l'interaction avec le paysage, traitent les détails avec soin, et utilisent de préférence des matériaux basiques.

Dieser dänische Architekt hat sein eigenes Büro eröffnet, nachdem er den Wettbewerb zum Bau des Arken Museums der Modernen Kunst in Kopenhagen gewann, das Projekt, das ihn in das internationale Panorama einreiht. Seine Werke artikulieren sich um Metaphern, die versuchen, eine Geschichte zu erzählen, wie die von einem Schiffbruch oder der Transformierung des Papiers in eine Zeitung. Die Entwürfe von Lund suchen die Interaktion mit der Landschaft, bewaren die Details und verwenden vorzugsweise grundlegende Materialien.

1962	Born in Copenhagen, Denmark.	*Naît à Copenhague, Danemark.*	Geboren in Kopenhagen, Dänemark.
1988	Emil Bissen Award from the *Royal Danish Academy of Fine Arts.*	*Prix Emil Bissen de la* Royal Danish Academy of Fine Arts.	Emil Bissen-Preis der *Royal Danish Academy of Fine Arts.*
1989	Completes his studies at the *Royal Danish Academy of Fine Arts.*	*Termine ses études à la* Royal Danish Academy of Fine Arts.	Beendet sein Studium, *Royal Danish Academy of Fine Arts.*
1991	Sets up the Søren Robert Lund, Architects, studio.	*Fonde l'agence* Søren Robert Lund, Architects.	Gründet das Büro *Søren Robert Lund, Architects.*
1994	Award from the Chicago *Artist International Scholarship.*	*Prix de la* Chicago Artist International Scholarship.	Preis des *Chicago Artist International Scholarship.*
1996	Nominated for the *Mies van der Rohe* Award.	*Nominé pour le prix* Mies van der Rohe.	Nominiert für den Preis *Mies van der Rohe.*
2002	*Eckersberg Medaillen* Prize from the *Royal Danish Academy of Fine Arts.*	*Prix Eckersberg Medaillen de la* Royal Danish Academy of Fine Arts.	*Eckersberg Medaillen*-Preis der *Royal Danish Academy of Fine Arts.*

Arken Museum of Modern Art

1996. Arken, Denmark.

In modern art museums, architecture dialogues directly with art which creates some interesting and at times ambiguous relationships. Arken's Museum of Modern Art is a synthesis of two tendencies which were developed in Scandinavia during the decades of the sixties, seventies and eighties. On the one hand, the project of Robert Lund draws on the influence of the "new empiricism" from Alvar Aalto, pursues spontaneity, and the adaptability of the building to traditional materials and to the place. It tries to recuperate domestic comfort, common sense, texture and color.

Dans les musées d'art moderne, l'architecture dialogue directement avec l'art, établissant des liens intéressants, et parfois ambigus. Le Musée d'Art Moderne d'Arken est une synthèse de deux tendances qui se développèrent en Scandinavie dans les années soixante, soixante-dix et quatre-vingt. Le projet de Robert Lund reprend l'influence du "nouvel empirisme" d'Alvar Aalto, quête de la spontanéité et de l'adaptabilité du bâtiment aux matériaux traditionnels et au lieu. Le projet veut réintégrer le confort domestique, le sens commun, la texture et la couleur.

In den Museen der Modernen Kunst führt die Architektur einen direkten Dialog mit der Kunst, um einige interesante und manchmal auch zweideutige Beziehungen zu schaffen. Das Museum der Modernen Kunst in Arken ist eine Synthese der zwei Tendenzen, die sich in Skandinavien während der 60er, 70er und 80er Jahre entwickelt haben. Das Projekt von Robert Lund greift den Einfluß des "Neuen Empirialismus" von Alvar Alto auf, daß die Spontanität, die Anpassungsfähigkeit des Gebäudes an die traditionellen Materialien und an den Ort verfolgt. Es versucht die häusliche Bequemlichkeiit wiederherzustellen, den Sinn für das Gemeinsame, die Textur und Farbe.

The building extends over the sand dunes and vegetation like a great horizontal body. Lund starts from the idea of a shipwreck to initiate the creative process.

Le bâtiment s'étend sur les dunes de sable et la végétation comme un grand corps horizontal. Lund part de l'idée d'un naufrage pour enclencher le processus créatif.

Das Gebäude breitet sich über die Sanddünen und die Vegetation wie ein großer horizontaler Körper aus. Lund geht von der Idee eines Schiffbruches aus, um den kreativen Prozeß zu initiieren.

Richard **Rogers**

SMALLCOUR EUROPÉENNE DES DROITS DE L'HOMME

Richard Rogers has converted the technological innovations used in his works into authentic aesthetic discourse, which has lead him to become one of the artificers of "High-Tech". Nonetheless, for Rogers, the new technologies are not only a way of expression but rather, they must be the key to achieving energy sustainability in the buildings. Defender of the city as the house of man, his theories advocate compact urban centers and designed for pedestrians.

Richard Rogers a converti les innovations techniques utilisées dans ses œuvres en véritable discours esthétique, faisant de lui l'un des artisans de l'architecture "High Tech". Néanmoins, pour Rogers, les nouvelles technologies ne sont pas seulement une forme d'expression, mais elles doivent être la clé de la durabilité énergétique des bâtiments. Défenseur de la ville comme maison de l'-homme, ses théories plaident pour des centres urbains compacts faits pour les piétons.

Richard Rogers hat die innovativen Techniken, die er in seinen Werken genutzt hat in einen wahren Ästhetik-Diskurs verwandelt, was ihn dazu gebracht hat, einer der Urheber der "High Tech" Architektur zu sein. Ohne Zweifel sind die neuen Technologien für Rogers nicht nur eine Ausdrucksform, sondern sie müssen der Schlüssel zur Erlangung der energetischen Aufrechterhaltung der Gebäude sein. Als Verteidiger der Stadt als Heimat des Menschen verteidigen seine Theorien kompakte und für Fußgänger gestaltete urbane Zentren.

1933	Born in Florence, Italy.	*Naît à Florence, Italie.*	Geboren in Florenz, Italien
1954-59	Studies in the *Architectural Association School* in London.	*Etudie à l'*Architectural Association School *de Londres.*	Studium an der *Architectural Association School* in London.
1963	Degree in architecture from the University of Yale.	*Diplôme d'architecte de l'Université de Yale.*	Abschluß als Architekt an der Universität von Yale.
1963	Founds *Team 4* studio with Norman Foster.	*Fonde l'agence* Team 4 *avec Norman Foster.*	Gründet das Büro *Team 4* mit Norman Foster.
1970	He associates with Renzo Piano.	*S'associe à Renzo Piano.*	Schließt sich mit Renzo Piano.
1977	Sets up *Richard Rogers Partnership.*	*Fonde* Richard Rogers Partnership.	Gründet *Richard Rogers Partnership.*
1983	Gold Medal from the *Royal Institute of British Architects.*	*Médaille d'Or du* Royal Institute of British Architects.	Goldmedallie des *Royal Institue of British Architects.*
1989	Arnold W. Brunner Prize from the *American Academy and Institute of Arts and Letters.*	*Prix Arnold W. Brunner de l'*American Academy and Institute of Arts and Letters.	Arnold W. Brunner Preis der *American Academy and Institute of Arts and Letters.*
2000	*Praemium Imperiale* from the *Japan Art Association.*	Praemium Imperiale *de la* Japan Art Association.	*Praemium Imperiale* der *Japan Art Association.*

COURT EUROPÉENNE DES DROITS DE L'HOMME

1995. Strasbourg, France.

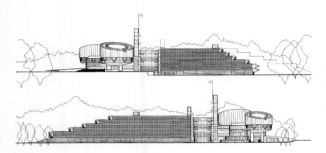

This project attempts to be the symbolic and program representation of the work of the internal organs of the Human Rights Tribune. Therefore, it is an open and transparent building which expresses the will to be transparent like the same justice.

The project, according to Rogers is an articulated complex of head and body, and both parts are connected by a vertical communications nucleus. The head, within this scheme, is the public part and in the tail or the body, to the contrary, can be found the administrative offices which support the institution.

Le projet prétend être la représentation symbolique et programmatique du rôle des organes internes de la Cour des Droits de l'Homme. Le bâtiment ouvert et transparent reflète la volonté de transparence de cette justice.

Selon Rogers, l'œuvre est un ensemble à la tête et au corps articulés, reliés par un noyau vertical de communications. Dans ce schéma, la tête est l'espace public, et à l'inverse, le corps héberge les dépendances administratives de l'institution.

Dieses Projekt versucht die symbolische und programatische Repräsentation der Arbeit der Internen Organe des Tribunals für Menschenrechte zu sein. Deshalb handelt es sich um ein offenes und transparentes Gebäude, daß den Willen dieser Justiz zur Transparenz ausdrückt.

Nach Rogers ist dieses Projekt ein artikulierender Komplex mit Kopf und Körper und beide Teile finden sich vereint um einen vertikalen Kommunikationskern. Der Kopf in diesem Schema ist der öffentliche Teil, im Schwanz oder Körper finden sich dagegen die Verwaltungsabteilungen, die die Institution unterstützen.

The dispersal of the different functions of the building into distinct
elements, the helps to attain a very
high level of integration of the
complex with the surroundings.

La désagrégation des différentes
fonctions du bâtiment en éléments
distincts facilite une excellente inté-
gration au paysage.

Die Zersplitterung der verschiede
nen Funktionen des Gebäudes ir
verschiedene Elemente begünstigt
daß die Integration in die Lanschaf
sehr hoch ist.

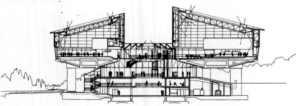

Kazuyo **Sejima**

PACHINKO PARLOR II
PACHINKO PARLOR III

For the architect Kazuyo Sejima, designing is a continuous process of discovery in which she searches to establish a theme which allows her to create something new where she can be in tune with her client's interests, the conditions of the terrain and her own ideas. Sejima understands architecture as a discipline which permits diagrams of spaces to be elaborated in order to describe in an abstract way the activities that will be developed in the place and as a means for understanding society better.

Pour l'architecte Kazuyo Sejima, le design est un processus continuel de découvertes. C'est la quête d'un thème qui permet la création de quelque chose de nouveau, capable de se conjuguer avec les intérêts du client, les conditions du terrain, et ses propres idées. Sejima conçoit l'architecture comme une discipline permettant d'élaborer des diagrammes d'espaces pour décrire d'une façon abstraite les activités d'un lieu. C'est également pour elle un moyen de mieux comprendre la société.

Für die Architektin Kazuyo Sejima ist das Entwerfen eines Projekts ein kontinuierlicher Prozeß der Entdeckung, in dem man ein Thema einführen will, das es erlaubt, etwas neues zu schaffen und das sich mit den Interessen der Kunden, den Bedingungen des Geländes und ihren eigenen Ideen dekken kann. Sejima versteht die Architektur wie eine Disziplin, die es erlaubt, Raumdiagramme zu entwickeln, um in abstrakter Form die ablaufenden Aktivitäten zu beschreiben, die sich an einem Ort abspielen und die als Mittel zum besseren Verständnis der Gesellschaft dienen.

1956	Born in Ibaraki, Japan.	*Naît à Ibaraki, Japon.*	Geboren in Ibaraki, Japan.
1981	Graduates from the *Japan Women's University.*	*Obtient le diplôme de la* Japan Women's University.	Abschluß an der *Japan Women's University.*
1981	Starts to work at the office of Toyo Ito.	*Travaille pour l'agence de Toyo Ito.*	Fängt im Büro von Toyo Ito an zu arbeiten.
1987	Sets up her own studio, *Kazuyo Sejima & Associates.*	*Fonde sa propre agence,* Kazuyo Sejima & Associates.	Gründet ihr eigenes Büro, *Kazuyo Sejima & Associates.*
1989	Yoshioka Award from the magazine *The Japan Architect.*	*Prix Yoshioka du magazine* The Japan Architect.	Yoshioka-Preis der Zeitschrift *The Japan Architect.*
1992	Young architect of the year Award from the *Japan Institute of Architects.*	*Prix du Jeune Architecte de l'Année du* Japan Institute of Architects.	Preis für den jüngsten Architekten des Jahres des Japan Institute of Architects.
1994	*Commercial Space Design Award '94* Grand Prize.	*Grand Prix* Comercial Space Design Award '94.	Großer Preis Comercial Space Design Award '94
1995	Kenneth F. Brown Prize from the University of Hawaii.	*Prix Kenneth F. Brown de l'Université d'Hawaï.*	Kenneth F. Brown-Preis der Universität von Hawai.

PACHINKO PARLOR II

1993. Naka, Ibaraki, Japan.

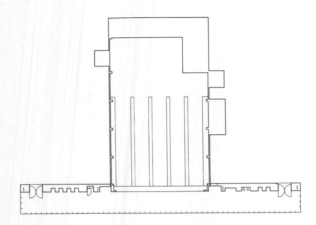

Pachinko is a very popular game in Japan which combines luck with skill. Pachinko Parlor II is a small intervention on a modest building in Naka, a provincial city. The purpose was to give it an entrance that would get both the pedestrian's attention and the motorists that go along the freeway. A facade with the absence of structure consisting only of great panes of glass that repeat the name of the establishment so that the letters displayed there become the sign of recognition from a distance.

Le Pachinko est un jeu très populaire au Japon qui combine hasard et adresse. Pachinko Parlor II est une petite intervention sur un modeste bâtiment de Naka, une ville de province. Il s'agissait de faire une entrée qui attire l'attention des piétons et des automobilistes empruntant l'autoroute. Le nom de l'établissement est reproduit sur l'ensemble de la façade exempte de structure et entièrement vitrée. Les lettres gravées deviennent ainsi un signe reconnaissable de loin.

Pachinko ist ein sehr populäres Spiel in Japan, das Zufall und Geschicklichkeit kombiniert. Pachinko Palor II ist ein kleiner Eingriff in ein bescheidenes Gebäude in Naka, einer Provinzstadt. Es handelt sich darum, ihm einen Eingang zu geben, der die Aufmerksamkeit des Fußgängers genauso auf sich zieht, wie die der Autofahrer, die auf der Autobahn daran vorbeifahren. Eine befreite Fassade mit einer Struktur, die nur aus großen Glaswänden zusammengesetzt ist, die den Namen des Unternehmens mit der Intention wiederholen, das die aufgenommenen Buchstaben sich in ein aus der Ferne leicht wiederzuerkennendes Zeichen verwandeln.

A yellow wall as a backdrop to glassy drapery, houses the ventilation apertures since none of the panels are movable.

Un mur jaune sert de toile de fond à la façade vitrée. Aucun de ses panneaux n'étant amovible, il est percé de voies d'aération du vestibule.

Eine gelbe Wand wie ein tiefer Vorhang aus glasiertem Tuch beherbegt die Hohlräume für die Klimaanlage in der Vorhalle, da keine seiner Paneelen begehbar ist.

Pachinko Parlor III

1996. Hitachiohta, Ibaraki, Japan.

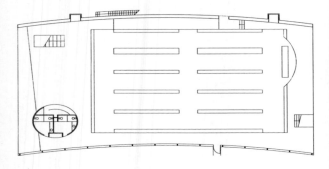

Pachinko III follows Pachinko II chronologically. Situated, also, in a provincial city, Hitachiohta, it occupies a large ground which extends to a freeway. Each of the volumes that make it up appear planted in the middle of the plot, forming strange archipelagos. Of the more than 4,000 square meters available, this small building barely occupies 700 square meters. The curvature of the facade and the use of light and the materials in such an attractive way that it was only necessary to have a modest sign displaying the name of the establishment.

Pachinko Parlor III suit le II chronologiquement. Egalement situé dans une ville de province, Hitachiohta, il occupe un vaste terrain donnant sur une autoroute. Chaque volume de l'ensemble se plante au centre du terrain, formant ainsi de curieux archipels. Des plus de 4.000 m² disponibles, ce petit bâtiment n'en occupe qu'à peine 700. La forme courbe de la façade et l'usage de la lumière et des matériaux offraient une publicité suffisante, en témoigne la modestie de l'enseigne de l'entreprise.

Pachinko Parlor III folgt zeitlich auf den II. Er liegt auch in einer Provinzstadt, Hitachiohta, belegt ein großes Grundstück direkt an der Autobahn, jedes der Gebäude, aus dem es besteht, scheint in der Mitte des Grundstücks zu stehen und formt merkwürdige Archipele. Auf den mehr als 4000 m², die zur Verfügung stehen, nimmt dieses kleine Gebäude kaum 700m² ein. Die Biegung der Fassade, die Nutzung des Lichts und die Materialien sind eine ausreichende Reklame, was nur eine schüchternen Buchstaben nötig macht, um den Namen der Einrichtung anzukündigen.

Bright, black strips outline colored, glass slits. During the day bright, black softly reflects the lights. At night, light from the interior cuts the strips that line the facade.

Des franges d'un noir brillant encadrent des fentes en verre coloré. Le jour, le noir brillant reflète doucement les lumières; la nuit, la lumière intérieure fait ressortir les franges qui recouvrent la façade.

Schwarzglänzende Fransen rahmen bunte Glasspalten ein. Tagsüber reflektiert ein glänzendes Schwarz leicht die Lichter, nachts strömt das Innenlicht auf die Fransen, die an der Fassade hängen.

Seth **Stein**

Seth Stein has made the search for essentiality into his own individual stamp. According to the architect himself, his work, considered minimalist, goes beyond this philosophy and pursues the purity of shape in order to create serene and refined spaces in which light, form and colors are the crucial elements. Stein, who rejects ornamentation in his designs, takes advantage of all the resources he has on hand so that the walls, closets, and furniture pass unnoticed when we do not need them.

Seth Stein a fait de la quête de l'essentialisme une empreinte personnelle. Selon l'architecte lui-même, ses œuvres, considérées comme minimalistes, dépassent le cadre de cette philosophie. Elles recherchent la pureté des formes dans l'objectif de créer des espaces sereins et raffinés, où la lumière, la forme et les couleurs jouent un rôle prépondérant. Dans ses réalisations, Stein rejette les ornementations, et utilise toutes les ressources dont il dispose pour créer des cloisons, des armoires et des meubles qui disparaissent lorsqu'ils ne sont plus utilisés.

Seth Stein hat der Suche nach dem Wesentlichen seinen eigenen Stempel aufgedrückt. Dem Architekten zufolge sind seine Arbeiten, die als minimalistisch angesehen werden, mehr in Richtung dieser Philosophie und verfolgen die Reinheit der Formen mit dem Ziel, klare und feine Räume zu schaffen, in denen Licht, Formen und Farben die entscheidenden Elemente sind. Stein, der Verzierungen in seinen Entwürfen vermeidet, nutzt alle Mittel in seiner Reichweite, damit Wände, Schränke und Möbel verschwunden bleiben, wenn wir sie nicht brauchen.

1959	Born in New York, U.S.A.	*Naît à New York, Etats-Unis.*	Geboren in New York, USA.
1985	Graduates from the *Architectural Association School* of London.	*Diplômé de l'Architectural Association School de Londres.*	Abschluss an der *Architectural Association School* in London.
1985-87	Works in the Richard Rogers studio.	*Travaille pour l'agence de Richard Rogers.*	Arbeitet im Büro von Richard Rogers.
1987-89	Works in the Norman Foster studio.	*Travaille pour l'agence de Norman Foster.*	Arbeitet im Büro von Norman Foster.
1989	Sets up his own office, *Seth Stein Architects* in London.	*Fonde sa propre agence, Seth Stein Architects, à Londres.*	Gründet sein eigenes Büro in London, *Seth Stein Architects*.

STEIN'S RESIDENCE

1996. Kensington, London, United Kingdom.

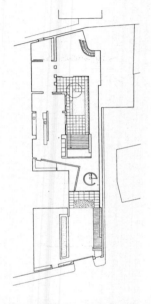

An old stable and a lot were adapted by Stein to project his own house. Stein does not propose a break with the existing building, nor therefore, with the typology and the traditional aspect of the constructions there. He prefers to act on the past, establish a dialogue and a continuity. The first condition is the conscientious restoration of all the existing buildings. With them, the new building will cohabitate.

Pour sa propre maison, Stein adapta une ancienne étable et son terrain. Il n'établit pas de rupture avec le bâtiment existant ni, par conséquent, avec la typologie et l'aspect traditionnel des constructions du lieu. Il préfère agir sur le passé, établir un dialogue et une continuité. La première démarche est la restauration méticuleuse de tous les bâtiments d'origine qui cohabiteront avec la nouvelle structure.

Ein alter Stall und ein Grundstück wurden von Stein angenommen, um sein eigenes Haus zu entwerfen. Stein wollte keinen Bruch mit dem existierenden Gebäude angehen, auch nicht mit der Typologie und dem traditionellen Aspekt der Bauwerke an dem Ort. Er bevorzugt, über der Vergangenheit zu handeln, einen Dialog und eine Kontinuität einzuführen. Die erste Bedingung ist die gewissenhafte Restaurierung aller existierender Gebäude. Mit ihnen wird die neue Struktur zusammenleben.

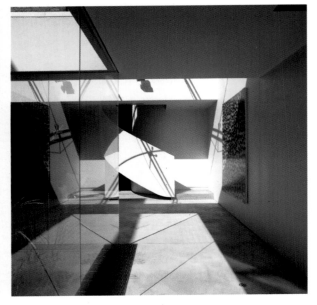

The patio interior is the central element of the project. It allows natural light to be introduced into all the essential spaces of the house and makes up the visual panorama.

Le patio intérieur est l'élément central du projet. Il permet d'introduire la lumière naturelle dans tous les espaces vitaux de la maison, et construit son panorama visuel.

Der Innenhof ist das zentrale Element des Projekts. Er erlaubt den Eintritt von natürlichem Licht in allen wesentlichen Räumen des Hauses und konstruiert sein visuelles Panorama.

The majority of the flooring of the house is pale gray concrete, finished manually so that it has the texture of orange skin.

La majeure partie du sol de la maison est en béton gris pâle, fini à la main pour lui donner un aspect peau d'orange.

Der größte Teil des Fußbodens des Hauses ist aus grauem blassen Beton, der manuell fertiggestellt wurde, um ihm einen ihm eine Orangenhauttextur zu geben.

Studio **Archea**

Laura Andreini, Marco Casamonti and Giovanni Polazzi are very closely involved in academic and research activity. The three of them are university professors and Casamonti even edits an architectural magazine (Area). When they founded their studio, they did it with the intention of experimenting in the field of architectural design from the most practical side. The fields in which they have worked range from the design of interiors to interventions in urban spaces.

Laura Andreini, Marco Casamonti et Giovanni Polazzi sont très investis dans la recherche et le monde académique. Ils sont tous trois professeurs d'université, et Casamonti édite même un magazine d'architecture (Area). Lorsqu'ils fondèrent leur agence, leur but était d'expérimenter dans le monde du design architectonique selon une orientation pratique. Les cadres de leurs projets vont du design intérieur à des interventions sur des espaces urbains.

Laura Andreini, Marco Casamonti und Giovanni Polazzi sind sehr mit dem akademischen Geschehen und der Forschung verbunden. Die drei sind Dozenten und Casamonti gibt eine Architekturzeitschrift heraus (*Area*). Als sie ihr Büro gegründet haben, haben sie das mit dem Willen getan, auf dem Gebiet des Architekturdesigns mit dem praktischsten Aspekt zu experimentieren.Die Bereiche, die ihre Projekte umfassen gehen vom Innendesign bis zu Eingriffen in die urbanen Räume.

	Laura Andreini, Marco Casamonti and Giovanni Polazzi obtained their architecture degree from the *Facoltà di Architettura* of the University of Florence.	*Laura Andreini, Marco Casamonti et Giovanni Polazzi obtiennent le diplôme d'architecte de la Facoltà di Architettura de l'Université de Florence.*	Laura Andreini, Marco Casamonti und Giovanni Polazzi haben den Titel der Architektur in der *Facoltà di Architettura* in der Universität von Florenz erhalten.
1988	Founded *Studio Archea Associati.*	*Fondent Studio Archea Associati.*	Gründen *Studio Archea Associati.*
1993	Requalification and appraisal of the Piazza della Vittoria in Castiglioncello.	*Requalification et estimation de la Piazza della Vittoria à Castiglioncello.*	Umwidmung und Aufwertung der *Piazza della Vittoria* in Castiglioncello.
1999	Third place in the international bid for the new main office of the *Istituto Universitario di Architettura* in Venice.	*Troisième place du concours international pour le nouveau siège de l'Istituto Universitario di Architettura de Venise.*	Dritter Platz im internationalen Wettbewerb für den neuen Sitz des *Istituto Universitario di Architettura* in Venedig.
2000	Second place in the international bid for the new headquarters of the *Agencia Spaziale Italiana* in Rome.	*Deuxième place du concours international pour le nouveau siège de l'Agencia Spaziale Italiana à Rome.*	Zweiter Platz im internationalen Wettbewerb für nden neuen Sitz der *Agencia Spaziale Italiana* in Rom.

Stop Line

1996. Curno, Bergamo, Italia.

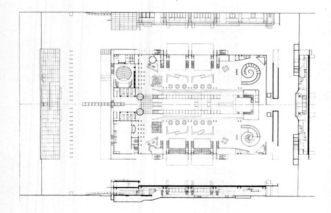

The exterior of Stop Line, cultural and recreation center, appears during the day as a forceful and hermetic volume, owing to its covering of Corten steel. At night, the orifices in the surface of the stainless steel become reticules of points of light. The building consists practically of only one unique space, with disengaged constructions that can be acceded to by means of ramps and stairs.

L'extérieur du centre culturel et de loisir Stop Line se présente le jour comme un volume contondant et hermétique, dû à son revêtement en acier Corten. La nuit, les orifices percés dans la plaque d'acier oxydé se transforment en une réticule de points lumineux. Le bâtiment se limite presque à un espace unique de constructions exemptes, auxquelles l'on accède par des rampes et des escaliers.

Das Exterior der *Stop Line*, Kultur- und Freizeitzentrum, präsentiert sich tagsüber aufgrund der Stahlverkleidung wie eine schlagkräftiges und verschlossenes Gebäude. Nachts, verwandeln sich die praktischen Öffnungen in der oxidierten Stahlplatte in ein Netz aus Lichtpunkten. Das Gebäude besteht praktisch aus einem einzigen Raum, mit freien Konstruktionen, die man über Rampen oder Treppen betritt.

The stairs, the ramps, the ventilation tubes and the beams that support the illumination, also are isolated as independent or sculptural elements.

Les escaliers, les rampes, les conduits d'aération et les rampes de spot sont également isolés comme éléments à part entière et sculpturaux.

Die Treppen, die Rampen, die Rohre der Klimaanlage und die Balken mit der Beleuchtung sind auch wie unabhängige oder bildhauerische Elemente isoliert.

Shin **Takamatsu**

The works of Shin Takamatsu have evolved from the roughness of his first works to futuristic designs, inspired in tools and machinery that incorporate more and more, light structures and flowing shapes. Takamatsu, who considers that architecture is like calligraphy because its strength does not lie in its structure, but rather, in the space that surrounds it, has adopted some elements of the minimalist language in order to endow some of his latest works with a climate of serene monumentality.

Depuis la rudesse de ses premières réalisations, les œuvres de Shin Takamatsu ont évolué vers des designs futuristes, inspirés par l'outillage et la machinerie, qui incorporent de plus en plus de structures légères et de formes fluides. Selon Takamatsu, l'architecture est comme la calligraphie, en cela qu'elle tire sa force non de la structure, mais de l'espace qui l'entoure. Il reprit certains éléments du langage minimaliste pour fournir à ses derniers ouvrages un climat de monumentalité sereine.

Die Werke von Shin Takamatsu haben sich seit der Rauheit seiner ersten Arbeiten zu futuristischen Entwürfen entwickelt, inspiriert von Werkzeugen und Maschinen, die jedes Mal leichtere Strukturen und flüssigere Formen aufnehmen. Takamatsu, der die Architektur als Kaligrafie betrachtet, weil seine Kraft nicht in der Struktur liegt, sondern im Raum, der sie umgibt, hat einige Elemente der minimalistischen Sprache entfernt, um seine letzten Arbeiten ein Klima von klarer Monumentalität zu geben.

1948	Born in Shimane, Japan.	*Naît à Shimane, Japon.*	Geboren in Shimane, Japan.
1971	Degree in architecture from the University of Kioto.	*Diplôme d'architecte de l'Université de Kyoto.*	Abschluß in Architektur an der Universität von Kioto.
1980	Founded *Shin Takamatsu, Architect & Associates*, in Kioto.	*Fonde Shin Takamatsu, Architect & Associates, à Kyoto.*	Gründet *Shin Takamatsu, Architect & Associates* in Kioto.
1984	Prize for young architects from the *Japan Association of Architects*.	*Prix pour jeunes architectes de la Japan Association of Architects.*	Jugendarchitekturpreis der *Japan Association of Architects*.
1985	Award from the *Biennale d'Architettura* in Venice.	*Prix de la Biennale d'Architettura de Venise.*	Preis der *Biennale d'Architettura* von Venedig
1989	Prize from the *Architectural Institute of Japan*.	*Prix de l'Architectural Institute of Japan.*	Preis des *Architectual Institute of Japan*.
1995	Honorary Member of the *American Institute of Architects*.	*Membre honoraire de l'American Institute of Architects.*	Ehrenmitglied des *American Institute of Architects*.
2001	Honorary Member of the *Royal Institute of British Architects*.	*Membre honoraire du Royal Institute of British Architects.*	Ehrenmitglied des *Royal Institute of British Architects*.

Shoji Ueda Museum of Photography

1995. Kishimoto-cho, Tottori, Japan.

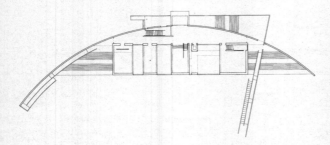

Shin Takamatsu integrates into this project the concept of *Ma*, which defines at the same time both a spatial and temporal interval. *Ma* is a pause, the silence between successive perceptions of the world and oneself, that continually vanish and are recreated.
Situated in bucolic surroundings with views of Daisen volcano, this museum consists of a sequence of four volumes of concrete alternated with three voids in which a surface of water is placed. Each volume has an exhibition space and they are illuminated by means of vertical and horizontal insicions.

Shin Takamatsu intègre dans ce projet le concept Ma, définissant un intervalle à la fois spatial et temporel. Ma est une pause, un silence entre des perceptions successives du monde et de moi-même, qui se dissipent et se recréent continuellement.
Situé dans un environnement bucolique donnant sur le volcan Daisen, ce musée est composé d'une séquence de quatre volumes en béton alternés par des vides, dans lesquels ont étés placées des surfaces d'eau. Chaque volume renferme un espace d'exposition, et est illuminé par des incisions verticales et horizontales.

Shin Takamatsu integriert in diesem Projekt das Ma-Konzept, welches gleichzeitig einen räumlichen und einen temporalen Intervall definiert. Ma ist die Pause, die Stille zwischen aufeinander folgelnden Wahrnehmungen der Welt und von dem was kontinuierlich ohnmächtig wird und sich vergnügt.
Dieses Museum, das sich in einer ländlichen Umgebung mit Blick auf den Vulkan Daisen befindet, besteht aus einer Sequenz von vier Betongebäuden, die sich mit drei Leeren, in denen eine Wasseroberfläche steht, abwechseln. Jedes Gebäude hat einen Austellungsraum und wird durch vertikale und horizontale Einschnitte beleuchtet.

The broken rhythm of the building, the succession of solids and voids, is inspired in the relationship between photography and reality. In the same way as the building, the photography shows fixed and cut images of reality.

Le rythme saccadé du bâtiment, la succession de pleins et de vides, s'inspire de la relation entre photographie et réalité. Tout comme le bâtiment, la photographie montre des images fixes et coupées de la réalité.

Der kurze Rhythmus des Gebäudes, die Folge von Volle und Leere ist von der Beziehung zwischen Photographie und Realität inspiriert. Ebenso wie das Gebäude zeigt das Foto starre und von der Realität gekürzte Bilder.

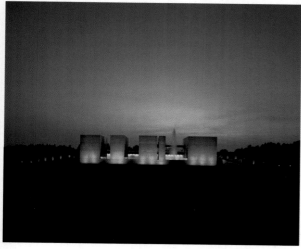

"There are two ways to relate architecture and nature: one consists of the search for harmony, and the other, to frame a scene by means of architecture. Here, we have adopted the second." (Shin Takamatsu).

"Il existe deux façons de relier architecture et nature: l'une consiste à rechercher l'harmonie, l'autre à planter un décor grâce à l'architecture. Dans ce cas, nous avons adopté la deuxième solution" (Shin Takamatsu).

"Es gibt zwei Arten, Architektur und Natur zu verbinden: Eine besteht aus der Suche nach Harmonie und die andere aus der Einrahmung eines Szenarios durch die Architektur. Hier haben wir die zweite genommen." (Shin Takamatsu).

TEN **Arquitectos**

COMEDOR PARA EMPLEADOS DE TELEVISA

CENTRO DE ARTE DRAMÁTICO

The work of "TEN Arquitectos" drinks from the waters of architectural rationalism although some of their works have compositions with geometric hybrids or uncompleted shapes. Influenced by their training in the U.S.A., both Enrique Norten and Bernardo Gómez-Pimienta take advantage of some of the principles of contemporary American architecture, but they do not adhere to the established currents and they move in a field of transition.

Les réalisations de "TEN Arquitectos" puisent aux sources du rationalisme architectonique, bien que certaines de leurs œuvres soient composées de géométries hybrides ou de formes incomplètes. Influencés par leur formation aux Etats-Unis, Enrique Norten et Bernardo Gómez-Pimienta reprennent certains principes de l'architecture contemporaine nord-américaine, sans pour autant adhérer à des courants établis, et évoluent dans le domaine de la transition.

Die Arbeiten der "TEN Architeckten" laben sich an den Quellen des architektonischen Razionalismus, auch wenn einige ihrer Werke Kompositionen mit hybriden Geometrien oder unvollendeten Formen haben. Beeinflußt durch ihre Ausbildung in den USA, nutzen sowohl Enrique Norten also auch Bernardo Gómez-Pimienta einige Prinzipien der nordamerikanischen Architektur, kleben aber nicht an etablierten Strömungen und bewegen sich auf dem Gebiet des Übergangs.

	Enrique Norten was born in Mexico City in 1954 and Bernardo Gómez-Pimienta in Brussels, Belgium, in 1961.	*Enrique Norten naît à Mexico, Mexique, en 1954, et Bernardo Gómez-Pimienta à Bruxelles, Belgique, en 1961.*	Enrique Norten ist 1954 in Mexiko Stadt geboren und Bernardo Gómez-Pimienta 1961 in Brüssel, Belgien.
	Norten has a degree from Universidad Iberoamericana in Mexico City and from Cornell, in New York. Gómez-Pimienta studied at the Universidad de Anáhuac, in Mexico City, and at Columbia in New York.	*Norten est diplômé de l'Universidad Iberoamericana de Mexico, et de celle de Cornell, New York. Gómez-Pimienta fit ses études à l'Université d'Anahuac de Mexico, et à celle de Columbia, New York.*	Norten hat einen Abschluß der Universidad Iberoamericana in Mexiko Stadt und Cornell, New York. Gómez-Pimienta hat an der Universität von Anáhuac, Mexiko Stadt und an der Columbia Universität in New York studiert.
1985	Norten founds TEN Arquitectos.	*Norten fonde TEN Arquitectos.*	Norten gründet *TEN Arquitectos*.
1987	Gómez-Pimienta joins TEN Arquitectos as co-director.	*Gómez-Pimienta devient codirecteur de TEN Arquitectos.*	Gómez-Pimienta kommt als Vize-Direktor zu *TEN Arquitectos*.
1993	First Prize at the Bienal de Arquitectura in Buenos Aires.	*Premier Prix de la Bienal de Arquitectura de Buenos Aires.*	Erster Preis der *Bienal de Arquitectura* von Buenos Aires.
1998	Mies van der Rohe Latinomericano Prize.	*Prix Mies van der Rohe Latino-Américain.*	Lateinamerikanischer Mies van der Rohe-Preis.

COMEDOR PARA EMPLEADOS DE TELEVISA

1993. México D.F., México.

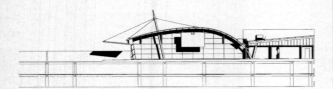

To understand this project, it is necessary to know two particular essential aspects: it deals with a space designed on a structure already existing and it is a building which is difficult to see from the exterior. This conditions the strategy of the project, whose most important decision is the choice of the hall of the restaurant to have a light roof which, with the facade, becomes one complete unit.

Pour comprendre ce projet, il est nécessaire de connaître deux particularités essentielles: c'est un espace élaboré sur une structure déjà existante, et le bâtiment est difficile à voir de l'extérieur. Ces éléments conditionnent la stratégie du projet, dont la plus importante décision fut de doter la salle de restaurant d'une toiture légère formant une unité avec la façade.

Um dieses Projekt zu verstehen, muß man man die essentiellen Einzelheiten kennen: es handelt sich um einen Raum, entworfen über einer bereits existierenden Struktur und von außen betrachtet ist es ein schwieriges Gebäude. Das bedingt die Strategie des Projekts, dessen wichtigste Entscheidung die Wahl für ein leichtes Dach, das eine Einheit mit der Fassade bildet, im Saal des Restaurant ist.

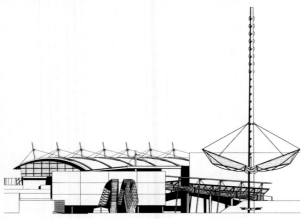

The profile is defined by the union of three roofs, which are independent, of which, only the largest (and central) is curved, whereas the others adapt to its dynamism by means of a slight inclination.

Le profil se définit par l'union de trois toitures indépendantes, la toiture principale et centrale étant courbée, alors que les autres s'adaptent à son dynamisme par une légère inclinaison.

Das Profil definiert sich durch die Union dreier unabhängiger Dächer, von denen nur das Hauptdach gebogen ist, während die anderen sich durch einen leichten Einschnitt an seine Dynamik anpassen.

Centro de Arte Dramático

1994. México D.F., México.

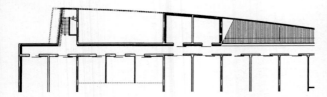

At an urbanistic level, the most important element is the great metal roof in the shape of a tube, supported by a structure of twelve round, steel tubes with isostatic supports at the ends, with tie rods that conform to all of the curve. Under the roof, a collection of volumes and planes contain and define the distinct elements that integrate the program.

D'un point de vue urbanistique, l'élément le plus important est la vaste toiture métallique de forme tubulaire, supportée par une structure de douze tubes d'acier arrondis aux appuis isostatiques aux extrémités, et tirants qui s'adaptent à l'ensemble de la surface courbée. Sous la toiture, un assortiment de volumes et de plans contiennent et définissent les différents éléments du programme.

Das wichtigste Element auf urbanistischer Ebene ist das große rohrförmige Metalldach, das von einer Struktur aus zwölf runden Stahlrohren mit isostatischen Stützen an ihren Enden, mit Zugankern, die sich auf der ganzen Strecke an die Rundung anpassen, getragen wird. Unter dem Dach eine Sammlung von Außenansichten und Plänen, die die verschiedenen Elemente beinhaltet und definiert, die das Programm integrieren.

The necessity to distribute 10,000 square meters of usable surface in a ground of 3,000 square meters made them design a series of stacked volumes, united by a great common space.

La nécessité de répartir 10.000 m² de surface utilisable sur un terrain de 3.000 m² explique l'empilement d'une série de volumes, unis par un vaste espace commun.

Die Notwendigkeit, 10000m² Nutzfläche auf einem Grundstück von 3000m² zu verteilen hat dazu geführt, daß eine Reihe von dicht gedrängten Gebäuden entworfen wurde, die sich durch einen großen gemeinsamen Platz vereinen.

The diverse architectural volumes are characterized by a different material (marble, wood, glass...)

Les divers volumes architectoniques se caractérisent par des matériaux différents (marbre, bois, verre...)

Die verschiedenen architecktonischen Außenansichten charakterisieren sich durch ein unterschiedliches Material (Marmor, Holz, Glas...)

Rafael **Viñoly**

The work of Rafael Viñoly maintains a structural originality that transcends current, passing, architectural trends. From his beginnings at the "Estudio de Arquitectura" until the present works of his firm in New York, Viñoly has always been concerned about rigor in the projects that he has undertaken, and he asserts that an architect must not only have creative inspiration, but rather, also, he must control the circumstances that surround the process of implementing a project.

L'œuvre de Rafael Viñoly garde une originalité structurale qui touche les modes passagères de courants architectoniques. Depuis ses débuts à l'Estudio de Arquitectura, jusqu'aux dernières réalisations de son agence de New York, Viñoly a toujours voulu traiter ses projets avec rigueur. Selon lui, l'architecte ne doit pas se contenter de son inspiration créatrice; il doit également contrôler tous les aspects du processus de réalisation d'un projet.

Die Arbeit von Rafael Viñoly erhält eine strukturelle Originalität aufrecht, die durch die Moden der vorrübergehenden architektonischen Strömungen durchsickert. Seit seinen Anfängen im "Estudio de Arquitectura" bis zu seinen letzten Werken seiner Firma in New York hat Viñoly sich immer um die Genauigkeit mit den Projekten, die er durchgeführt hat, gekümmert und bestätigt, daß ein Architekt nicht nur kreative Inspiration haben muß, sondern er muß auch die Umstände kontrollieren, die den ganzen Durchführungsprozeß eines Projektes mitreißen.

1944	Born in Montevideo, Uruguay.	*Naît à Montevideo, Uruguay.*	Geboren in Montevideo, Uruguay.
1969	Graduates from the Faculty of Architecture and Urbanism from the Universidad de Buenos Aires.	*Diplômé de la Facultad de Arquitectura y Urbanismo de l'Université de Buenos Aires.*	Abschluss an der *Facultad de Arquitectura y Urbanismo,* Universität von Buenos Aires.
	Co-founder of the Estudio de Arquitectura, in Argentina.	*Confondateur de l'Estudio de Arquitectura, Argentine.*	Mitbegründer des *Estudio de Arquitectura* in Argentinien
1979	Moves to New York.	*Déménage à New York.*	Umzug nach New York.
1983	Sets up Rafael Viñoly Architects.	*Fonde Rafael Viñoly Architects.*	Gründet *Rafael Viñoly Architects.*
1993	Member of the *American Insitute of Architects.*	*Membre de l'American Institute of Architects.*	Mitglied des *American Institute of Architects.*
1994	*Excellence in Design* Award from the *New York State Association of Architects.*	*Prix Excellence in Design de la New York State Association of Architects.*	Excellence in Design-Preis von der *New York State Association of Architects.*
	Member of the *Japan Institute of Architects.*	*Membre du Japan Institute of Architects.*	Mitglied des *Japan Institute of Architects.*

TOKYO INTERNATIONAL FORUM

1997. Tokyo, Japan.

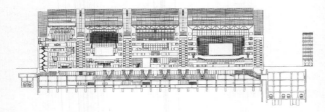

The proposal of this project, from the very beginning, opted to dispersing the most important parts of the program into differentiated volumes. On one side four halls for concerts, exhibitions and congresses. To the west, they adapt to the urban setting, escalade by sizes and united by a common facade which connects it to the city. The 57 meter-high wall curtain is made up of panels of 16 mm. thick laminated glass, stabilized throughout by an auxiliary, bracing structure which is adequate for good performance in case of earthquakes.

Dès le début, le projet tendait vers une désagrégation des parties les plus importantes du programme en volumes différenciés. Côté ouest, quatre grandes salles de concert, exposition et congrès, s'adaptent à la trame urbaine de l'environnement, se superposant par taille, et s'unissant par une façade commune donnant sur la ville. Le mur rideau de 57 m de hauteur est composé de panneaux de verre laminé de 16 mm d'épaisseur. Il est maintenu par une structure auxiliaire tendue, et conçu pour offrir une bonne résistance aux tremblements de terre.

Der Vorschlag dieses Projekts ging vom vom ersten Augenblickin Richtung Zerstreuung der wichtigsten Teile des Programms in differenzierten Gebäuden. Auf der einen Seite vier große Säle für Konzerte, Ausstellungen und Kongresse im Osten, die sich an die urbane Handlung der Umgebung durch Größe anpassen und sich durch eine gemeinsame Fassase mit der Stadt vereinen. Die Stützmauer von 57m Höhe besteht aus 16 mm starken laminierten Glaspaneelen, stabilisiert mit einer Hilfsstruktur und erdbebensicher.

In the interior of the great atrium, catwalks and braces reinforce the fine, glass curtain structure.

A l'intérieur du vaste atrium, des passerelles et tirants rigidifient la fine structure du pan de verre.

Im Inneren des großen Atriums versteifen Brücken und Zuganker die feine Struktur des Glasabschnitts.

Créditos **fotográficos** / Referenze **fotografiche** / Fotógrafos

J. Apicella, P. Follet/C.P. & A.: *Petronas Towers* • Richard Barnes: *Fukuoka Housing* • Behnisch & Partner, Christian Kandzia: *Deutscher Bundestag* • Tom Bonner: *Residence Lawson, The Box* • Friedrich Busam / Architekturphoto *Konferenzpavillon Vitra, Arken Museum of Modern Art, Court Européenne des Droits de l'Homme, New Trade Fair. Leipzig* • Ramón Camprubí, David Cardelús, Iván Bercedo: *L'Illa Diagonal, San Francisco Museum of Modern Art* • David Cardelús: *Centro Cultural de Sant Cugat* • Richard Davies: *Stein's Residence* • Michel Denancé, George Fessy: *Bibliothéque Nationale de France* • Georges Fessy: *Centre Technique du Livre Marne la Vallée* • M.Fujitsuka: *Water / Glass* • Katsuaki Furudate, Yoshio Takase: *Kyoto Concert Hall* • Dennis Gilbert: *Haus in Deutschalnd* • Luis Gordoa: *Comedor para empleados de Televisa, Centro de Arte Dramático* • Eduard Hueber: *Haus Häusler, Betriebsgebäude Holz-Altenried, Betriebsgebäude Lagertechnik Wolfurt* • Timothy Hursley: *Denver Central Library, University of Cincinnati Engineering Center* • Biblioteca Pública de la Meseta: *Tokyo International Forum* • Yasuhiro Ishimoto, Katsuaki Furudate, Yoshio Takase: *Japanese Art Center in Cracow* • Taizo Kurukawa, Osamu Murai, César Pelli, Yukio Yoshimura: *Sea Hawk Hotel* • Lourdes Legorreta: *Biblioteca Central Monterrey, Edificio de oficinas en Monterrey* • Lourdes Legorreta, Paul Bardagjy: *San Antonio Library* • Lock Images: *Centraal Beheer* • Mitsuo Matsuoka, Kaneaki Monma, Cesar Pelli: *NTT Headquarters Building* • Fujitsuka Mitsumasa: *Yusuhara Visitor's Center* • Nacasa & Partners Inc.: *Pachinko Parlor II, Pachinko Parlor III, Shoji Ueda Museum of Photography* • Shigeo Ogawa: *Chikatsu-Asuka Historical Museum* • Tomio Ohashi: *Nagaoka Lyric Hall, Wakayama Museum* • Eugeni Pons: *Museo Guggenheim de Bilbao* • Christian Richters: *Maastricht Housing, Faculty of Economics and Management, Fondation Cartier pour l'art Contemporain, Vroom & Dreesman Shopping Center, Renovation and extension Rijksmuseum, Nature Museum. Rotterdam, School for Fashion and Graphic Industry* • Ralph Richter / Architekturphoto: *Gare TGV Lyon-Satôlas* • Phillipe Ruault, Ralph Richter: *Triangle de Gares. Euralille* • Eric Saillet: *Le Sémaphore* • Pietro Savorelli, Saverio Lombardi Vallauri: *Stop Line* • Musao Sudo, Shinkenchiku-sha: *Republic Plaza* • Hisao Suzuki: *Domus. Casa del Hombre* • Jussi Tiainen: *Foibe Housing and Amenity Center for Seniors Citizens, Finnish Embassy in Washington D.C.* • Bill Timmerman: *Temple Kol Ami, Riddell's* • Herman H. van Doorn: *Faculty of Law, University of Cambridge* • Paul Warchol: *Makuhari Housing, Chapel of St.Ignatius* • Wenzel: *Stockholm Museum of Modern Art* • Gerald Zugmann, Hélène Bisnet: *Forschungszentrum Seibersdorf*